Grieving Us

Also by Kimberley Pittman-Schulz

Mosslight

GRIEVING US

A Field Guide
for Living With Loss
WITHOUT LOSING
YOURSELF

KIMBERLEY PITTMAN-SCHULZ

ISBN: 978-1-7365052-0-5 paperback

Author's Note
Aspects of many characters and their personal stories have been altered
to protect their privacy and the often deeply personal nature of their losses, especially the stories of donors and colleagues with whom I've worked.
I've changed their names, identifying characteristics, and contextual details, in some cases merging the similar stories of two people into one to
assure anonymity. Their words are shared as I remember them, and all
stories are true to the extent memory allows.

Seeking Help
This book is intended to be a self-help resource in your personal journey with loss, grief, healing, and achieving well-being. It is not meant to
replace professional medical or mental health care. If you are struggling
with extreme grief and/or experiencing suicidal thoughts, please seek
immediate professional support. The world needs you to live your one-
and-only, precious life.

Book Cover Design
Daliborka Mijailovic

Interior Book Design
Alejandro Martin

Dedication

In memory of Pammy and Kathy
Where are you now?
Who would you be if you were still here?
You are the loss that comes along with me.

With empathy for My Parents
We cried, but we also laughed.
You are now nestled with your two girls.
I miss you, yet you are still with me.

With gratitude to Terry
You taught me the birds, and one day,
sooner than we'd like, you will take flight.
Love you, SilverBear.

Download Your Free Copy
of the Audiobook.

As my thank you for purchasing this book, please accept a free copy of the audio version.It includes bonus resources to help you implement the practices shared in **Grieving Us**. Grieving is not an easy process. Sometimes even reading can be draining.

Let me read this book to you.

Download your audiobook at my website:
https://gifts.poetowl.com/grieving-us-audiobook

Table of Contents

Introduction

Loss comes along. First it breaks your heart,

then it stays.

Digging in the garden, I plucked loose a smooth river rock where I wanted to bury flower roots, a nasturtium with edible, fiery-orange blossoms. A river rock, yet no river in sight. How did that get here?

A long history precedes you and me. We all grow out of what has come and gone.

Gone. It's one syllable that sounds so final, doesn't it? So many people and animals I've loved are *gone.* I suspect that's true for you, too. Is that why you're here? Welcome to this book. It's about learning to live with loss and with joy in a world missing someone you love.

Life holds surprises.

My garden must have been a rush of water once. Now it's redwoods, a house, and land visited by wildlife from quail to bears, two indoor kitties, my husband who's navigating the end of his life, and me sometimes holding a palm full of nasturtium roots.

The river rock wasn't the surprise. When I moved the rock, there was a flowing current, but it wasn't water, it was pill bugs. Do you know what pill bugs are? They're tiny, about the size of your pinky fingernail, and they have armadillo backs and roll into a tiny ball if you touch them. They're also called roly-polys. These were frantic. I imagined them sighing, *pesky human!* Most were dark brown like coffee grounds or grey as the stone I'd just lifted away. But. Among the scattering mass, surprise, there were three bright lavender pill bugs. *Lavender!* Beautiful *lavender.*

Know what popped into my head then? *Mama.* I wanted to show her the lavender pill bugs. But she's been dead for years. *Gone.*

Pill bugs have always fascinated me, but my mother could do without them. They were to be avoided as she worked in her garden, barefoot and ungloved. My mind went on a journey about how my mother could learn to admire a humble pill bug if she saw these lavender ones. Remembering my mother, a wave of emotion built, a boomerang of grief. I felt the heat of tears in my eyes as I kneeled in dirt.

Memory is a blessing and a burden. You ever feel that way?

Death happens. It happens to the people we love and to our beloved animal companions. It will happen to me and to you. Then if we're loved, we'll be the source of others' pain.

When you're grieving, a stack of sympathy cards tell you how your loved one will live on in your heart and memories. It's true. My mother

2

being with me in the soil and surprise of lavender pill bugs is living proof, or not-so-living proof, that she's still with me.

To say that death changes a relationship, however, is the greatest understatement on this planet. Exactly how do I text my mother a photo of the lavender pill bugs? Regardless what you or I believe of the afterlife, our loved ones are gone as a physical, breathing presence in our lives. Forever.

How do I live with loss without losing myself?

When other women talk to me about loss and feeling stuck in grief, that's the number one question they ask. They're not really asking *me*, as if I can fix them. Mostly they're asking themselves or God or a sky full of dull clouds or as I've done, my kittens, technically cats now, who can only cock their heads, quietly confused.

The goal is to keep loss, or more specifically the vast range of grief emotions that accompany it, from consuming your life in all its meaning, purpose, and beauty. The world needs you to live your one, unique, beautiful-if-heart-broken life. No kidding.

Unfortunately, feelings of despair, longing, anxiety, anger, regret, emptiness, and a sense of being utterly lost can bring your life to an abrupt halt. You'll look around, astounded, that the world keeps on going, people doing what they've always done, the sun rising and setting, all as if nothing happened. But. Something *did* happen. Death visited.

Once family and friends have shared their condolences, they move on, often expecting you to do the same. You can feel very alone. Grief is unavoidable when someone you love dies. Grief is part of healing and helping you figure out how to hold your beloved someone in your life in a new way. Sometimes, though, grief can become an overwhelming presence, as if you're falling down a giant hole or bottomless well. It's hard to imagine ever climbing out, let alone smiling.

Is that what grief is like for you? What if you could take a *break* from grief?

This book is for you, to help you get that break and experience joy again. Right now, believe joy is there with you waiting to emerge.

Imagine taking a break from being deeply sad or totally numb. In that break, you feel light. Literally, your body feels freed, as if you took off a backpack full of rocks. You also feel *the* light. The sun is coming through those dull clouds, the brightness of the world finding you among the nearly eight billion people on the planet. It's a day and a world you know you are meant to be in. Imperfect? Yes. But you feel good anyway.

What if little by little that break got bigger and bigger? I can show you how to create that break from grief and cultivate joy in your life every day. Yes, really.

Loss is life-changing.

Loss is the one powerful force that's shaped my life. I know I'm not unique in having a lifetime of people I love die. For me, it started early, at age three and a half, surviving a house fire that my sisters, sleeping in the same room, did not. My mother was never the same after that, which is another kind of loss. I witnessed her pain for the rest of her life. Not looking for sympathy here. I'm just saying, it is what it is.

Over time, I lost both parents to lung cancer, a mother-in-law who adored me, friends to suicide, a first love and a former husband to illness-es, a snaggle-toothed dog, and four sweet-spirited cats. I've been stunned

4

at how some losses knocked me completely off center, while others I seemed to navigate just fine.

The death of my mother hit me the hardest, but then, we had a complicated relationship. It took more than two years to get my life moving forward without my mother. I changed jobs more than once, the simplest chores seemed impossible, and in the middle of it all, my father was declining toward his death.

While I now know it's not unusual, but common, to be in what I call *loss limbo*, I wish I had found a way through that awful time sooner. Back then a few people and my physician suggested antidepressants, which can work for some. I knew, however, that for me, deep, unrelenting grief was fundamentally different than depression. Counseling, or "talk therapy," helped a little. It was good to understand the five stages of grief. However, I could go through all five stages in a morning!

Honestly, those approaches didn't lead to well-being. There was no "how to" get better that really gave me an actionable set of steps or process for getting *unlost* from loss.

I needed to shape my own healing path.

My hope in writing this book is that it will help you shorten the time you spend in pain and the darkest moods of grief. By sharing my life-support system for living with loss—the rituals, habits, and mindsets that really work—I want you to avoid *loss limbo.*

It's not about pushing grief away or rushing through it. Trying to sidestep grief is a common response, and a mistake, that can lengthen the time you spend in distress, trust me. My approach focuses on harnessing loss so unrelenting grief doesn't take away, as poet Mary Oliver calls it, "your one wild and precious life."

Now my husband is in his end-of-life time. So, I know loss lies both behind me and ahead of me. It's with me now in the form of anticipatory grief. Heart disease has already taken so much from my husband, from us. His approaching death is undeniable.

Beyond learning to live with the deaths of so many I've loved, I've worked with hundreds of individuals and families in my professional role as a charitable and end-of-life planning advisor and leader for 25+ years. I've led or worked for a range of philanthropic organizations (from community-based to international), which sometimes includes entering deeply intimate, one-to-one conversations.

It's been an unexpected gift to be a listening ally and a resource to people from strikingly diverse backgrounds as they consider the meaning of their lives. I've sat with them as they acknowledged the reality of death, shared their losses and regrets, sharpened their focus on living, and thoughtfully shaped their personal legacy, including the values they'd leave behind. Occasionally, we cried together. Other times, we found ourselves laughing so hard our ribs hurt, because, as I've learned, laughter is always there, jumping out unexpectedly from the shadows of despair, if we let it.

I'm also a poet, writer, naturalist, and mentor who strives to expand awareness and empathy so this planet will be more livable for all beings, especially in a time of heightened racial and cultural divide and an era where we're losing entire species daily.

We're living with huge communal loss right now. Add in a pandemic as I write, and we have global grief.

Becoming an expert in death and loss hasn't been my goal.

I'm here as a fellow traveler who has more experience dealing with death and dying than I'd like. My intention is to come alongside you to share what works for me. I'm still evolving and discovering the diverse faces of loss, grief, and mourning as I work on becoming the best version of me possible.

This book takes you on a practical, step-by-step journey to build your own, unique life-support system for living with loss. There are four progressive stages to achieving greater well-being and joy, so I've broken the book into four sections. Each section comprises a few chapters that combine sharing concepts and strategies with storytelling to illustrate ideas, including what has and hasn't worked for others or myself. At the end of each section there's a Practice Chapter with how-to guidance to implement the concepts and strategies into your process of mourning and building a new post-loss life.

In Section One, we'll review the big ideas of loss, grief, mourning, and becoming, including the importance of telling your Loss Story. Then I'll offer a process for how you might tell your Loss Story and set a Feeling Intention to imagine and define a near future where you're enjoying a true sense of well-being.

In Section Two, we'll explore your senses and the way in which your body can reconnect you to your life, while touching on the impact of relationships in shaping your identity and grief experience. I'll show you how to start a single tiny, sensory ritual to create a break from grief that's doable, even if you're feeling exhausted, detached, too busy or overwhelmed, or otherwise unable to accomplish anything.

Small victories add up to transformation. In Section Three, we'll spend time with joy and your capacity to cultivate it in your daily life, then we'll discuss the power of action and focusing your attention to move your life forward. You'll learn how to build a flexible Joy Habit, if you don't already have one, and give yourself space to play, even if just a few minutes a day.

Moving into Section Four, we'll work on expanding and deepening your break from grief by shifting existing mindsets or developing new ones, while learning how to leverage memory and meaning as part of your healing. Finally, I'll provide a framework for building an Emotional Flak Jacket, a mindset toolbox, if you will, and discuss possible next steps in your journey to live with loss *and* with joy.

Let me make two final points about this book. First, it isn't for everyone. If you are in the early, raw stages of grief, this book may be for you—just not yet. Because I'll be asking you to focus on your senses, memories, and sources of meaning, you may not be ready for the practices and approaches I'm sharing. Put the book aside and come back to it when you're ready. At the same time, there are many viable approaches to working through grief and getting your life back on solid footing. What works for one person may or may not work for another. If you need a different approach, please pass this book on to someone else struggling with loss who may benefit.

Second, you don't have to live in the woods or hang out with ravens for the strategies I suggest to work. I'm a bit of a nature and natural history geek who thrives in forests and paddling lagoons, so examples often have a wild or rural context. If you're a city dweller, you could think of the stories as a loss camping retreat, if that helps. Regardless, all of the concepts and practices outlined will work if you're sitting in the middle of a dense urban environment, hanging out in a comfy suburb, enjoying small-town life, or isolating as a hermit. Just have an open mind and try the practices.

Kindred spirits are found in unlikely places.

Are you wondering what happened that day as I crouched beside a hole with lavender pill bugs and the white-lightning roots of a nasturtium waiting to be planted? After a little cry, I said to myself, "Miss you, Mama," followed by, "that's enough." I grinned, remembering how my mother used to say, "Talking to yourself is the only way to get an intelligent answer." She was funny.

I couldn't help gently touching one of the little buggy beings. It curled into a minute, armored ball, briefly immobile, then straightened out and burrowed with its 14 hair-like legs under pebbles. Focused only on paying attention to the moment—each detail of movement, color, texture, and feeling—I savored it all.

Good news. That boomerang of grief didn't take away my day. My life-support system worked for me, just as my roly—poly friend's defense system worked for it.

Finally, curiosity—another practice that keeps me out of emotional potholes—got the better of me. I hit the Internet to learn more about the lavender color of those three pill bugs. First, I was reminded that pill bugs are crustaceans rather than bugs or insects, meaning they're related to crabs and lobsters, though I'm not planning to serve one up with butter any time soon. Moisture-lovers, no wonder they were hanging out with a river rock.

And the lavender? Turns out, the lavender is a sign that those roll-pol-ys were infected by a virus. With this experience happening during our COVID-19 pandemic, I felt a kinship to those teeny crustaceans. How handy it would be if our novel corona virus turned people lavender when infected. Testing problem solved! The kinship, though, goes deeper than viruses.

All beings battle to live and to live with death.

Section 1

Death visited. Now what?

1

Storytelling

Your Loss Story is a bridge back to you

It's not gravity that grounds us, keeps us from spinning off into the black, night sky. It's love stories. Some of them are happy, others hard. Love isn't always kind, though it wants to be. Even in death, the story says, I love you still.

— from my notebooks, August 2003

Red. My first loss is lodged in my mind as color. When I woke one early-October night to fire in the doorway, it was red. I crawled out of my sheets on the bottom of a bunk bed and tried waking my big sister, six years old, on the top, but couldn't. Smoke snaked up and pooled at the ceiling above her. My baby sister, who turned two that day, her birthday, was standing up in her crib near the door. Shaking the rails, she was trying to climb out, chattering something that I couldn't hear, because, as I realize now, fire eating a house is loud.

I went to the window where I saw flashes of red. Outside, people were looking at me—my mother crying in her nightgown, the next-door neighbor I called Auntie, and others, too. Red light was pulsing and splashing across their faces as a fire truck approached. The windowpane was warm as I pounded with open hands at the glass. "Out," I was calling.

The eyes take in so much that the mind often latches onto strange details, like crayons on the floor. I was looking at a red one I'd broken earlier that day that made my big sister mad at me, just as my father punched his bare fist through the window. He scraped shards of glass from the sill and pulled me into his arms, more red, his blood in his palms, then on me. I was handed off to the group of watchers, and I remember being kissed as my father ran back to the house. Then we all froze, hearing an explosion inside. It was one of the few times my father openly sobbed, letting loose a howling, unforgettable sound.

This is the hardest fact: Some of us get to keep on living, and some of us don't.

Death, loss, survival. They're not words. They're more visceral, as if the architecture of my body, tissues to bone, my very cells, grieve. Decades have passed, and still, when this snippet of memory visits me, it's as if some invisible hand has reached inside with a crushing grip.

If you are here with me in this moment, the two of us brought together by this book, I think you understand what I am saying. If we were together physically, I'd ask, "Do you want to tell me about your loss?" I would listen. It's important to tell your Loss Story. You need to tell it, more than once and over time.

Why tell your Loss Story?

We are our stories. They connect us to ourselves and to others. Telling them is proof that we exist and that we are on a journey that hasn't ended yet. When someone hears our Loss Story, really listens to it, they connect with us in the most human way.

I was especially struck by the power of loss storytelling when I traveled in Sierra Leone in 2013 as part of my work in the international child development sphere. It's a country of deep loss due to a war and poverty, then an Ebola outbreak in 2014. As I visited villages, it was through shared stories that I came to connect personally with so many individuals and communities.

There was a custom of first meeting with the local leader called the Paramount Chief, or if a woman, the Mammy Chief, to be received and invited into a village. They would explain their relationship to a clan and their tribal roots, then share what was meaningful to their people, talk about their talents then their challenges, and finally discuss what they wanted for their children. Then they asked the same of me. They never inquired about my job, but they listened intensely to my story as I had to theirs.

Part of the custom in meeting a Chief was to bring a modest gift or token amount of money in the local currency. Well, in my culture, thanks Mother, money (flat and packable!) is deemed helpful but less thoughtful than a well selected gift. As I prepared for the three-week journey through Sierra Leone and parts of Liberia, I needed to travel light in these developing countries with mostly red-mud roads, almost no electricity, and simple "guest houses" to sleep in each night.

At the same time, I wanted something that represented my home in the southernmost stretch of the Pacific Northwest, something symbolic to me that would nurture real cultural exchange. I ended up taking two-ounce foil pouches of wild salmon, and since I wasn't sure how many chiefs I'd meet, I had a duffel bag full of salmon. As I checked it at the airport, I thought, *hang on for the mother of all migrations.* We'd travel nearly 7,000 miles. I imaged the currents of air instead of water they'd fly through, my school of silvery salmon pouches.

Each time I sat down with a Chief, when it came time to present my salmon offering, I was asked its meaning. I explained that for those of us in the Pacific Northwest, salmon are central to the balance of our natural environment and culture, especially for our native people, but also for those of us who choose to live there. I explained how salmon are amazing anadromous fish, that is, how they are born in freshwater streams, then swim out and live their lives in the salty ocean, then swim back up into those streams they came from to lay and fertilize their eggs and make the next generation. They die where they were born, and their bodies literally feed the river, the land it passes through, and their babies.

I shared how, when I lived along a river, we waited for and celebrated the return of the salmon and how saddened I am by the serious decline in salmon populations because we're not taking good care of our planet. The salmon teach us about surviving in all conditions, fresh or salty, fighting against predators and stormy tides to get home.

They remind us, I said, that we can always return home at the end of a journey. As my words came out of my mouth, inspired and excited about being in Sierra Leone, I also felt far from home in distance and differentness. I thought, *I know how you feel, salmon, that drive to leave and the pull to return home.*

So here's the power of story and how so many stories are stories of loss. The very first Chief I met was an elder, and his eyes became shiny as I spoke, as if holding back tears. Thinking I had somehow upset or offended this Chief, I glanced at my new friend and colleague, Fataba, who was guiding me during this trip. I gave her my best "help-me!" look. Before she could say anything, the Chief took my hand and thanked me. Then, I suppose seeing my puzzled face, he explained his emotion.

At the time I was visiting Sierra Leone, it had not yet been 10 years since a bloody civil war, which killed over 50,000 and maimed even more. I met several people missing hands or entire arms, and some who greeted me smiling through severe facial scars where they'd been slashed with a machete, or as they call it there, a cutlass, during the war. In fact, whenever I mention my time in Sierra Leone to another American, if someone even knows where the country is (West Africa), then they immediately think of the movie *Blood Diamonds* and wince.

The Chief explained that during the war, millions fled the country seeking safety, including him and most in his village. He shared how the deep longing for home and for the way things used to be were intense as refugees. I could see and feel how even years later, back in their homeland and talking with me, this man's longing and loss were still raw.

He said that my story of the salmon, reminding him of the hope and power of returning home, deeply touched him, and that it "makes us one." Then I was fighting emotion. This experience happened so many times as I moved through the rural up country of Sierra Leone.

On that trip, I witnessed something new: communal grief. It's when an entire community shares a deep loss. I also witnessed stunning resilience.

Can you imagine a nation of people confronted with true atrocities, Kalashnikovs and machetes cutting through families, everyone fleeing in search of safety, hiding in other countries, and returning to villages that, if not burned to a black smudge, were filled with horrific memories?

When I asked Fataba, who had also fled and returned, how she dealt with the loss and grief, she said, "Everyone knows death, so you are never alone. We would tell each other our stories. They were different but also the same, and you feel better for awhile."

Your Loss Story is a bridge to what's next.

In a way, when someone you love dies, it's as if you've been sent on a trip that you can never really come home from. Like the families I met in Sierra Leone, when you do come back to what you think of as home, it's a different place and you make a new life there.

Telling your Loss Story is a way of building a bridge. Yes, the telling is a bridge between you and others, because as Fataba pointed out, everyone is touched by death. But there's a more important audience: You.

Whenever you tell your story, you are honoring your very real, if uninvited, loss and your survival. Your voice and mind and body and emotions as you speak, they all help you move from the life you knew when your loved one was in the world to a new world where you get to live but have to do it without them.

Telling your Loss Story is also a kind of pressure valve. When you do it, as Fataba said, you feel better, at least for a while, which is why your story needs to be told more than once. Even if you can barely talk through your tears, when it's been spoken, there's been a little healing. The funny thing about telling a Loss Story is that you hang on to it fiercely and let it go at the same time.

Loss is abundant that way. You can never get rid of it, just lighten your load for awhile. When you intentionally tell your Loss Story, you get better at navigating the diversity of feelings and physical reactions. You get to mourn and move forward.

Most importantly, you reduce the likelihood that your Loss Story will ambush you. What do I mean? Have you ever fallen apart unexpectedly and inconveniently?

If you keep your Loss Story closed off in some dark closet of your heart, it will burst through the door and surprise you, and maybe others. You'll find yourself in a meeting or dinner with friends suddenly wailing into your coffee, because your Loss Story wants to be told. Your pain needs attention and will push itself out into the world without asking you, *is now a good time?*

Please know, it's okay to fall apart—no need to be embarrassed or apologetic. It will just happen, sometimes years or decades after a death. Been there, done that. Still, I know that for me and many others struggling to get out of loss limbo, having some moderate amount of control over when our Loss Story is shared is a helpful early step in getting our lives back.

Telling your Loss Story is also an expression of love itself. Remembering our loved ones is how we affirm to ourselves and the universe that their lives made, and still make, a difference.

One of my goals in traveling to Sierra Leone was to meet two children that I sponsored there, Thaimo and Alie, in a region called Bandankoro. After my mother and then my father died, I funded the building of a very humble but needed two-room school in memory of my parents. So many schools were demolished during the war, because every war includes some attack on education and culture.

After the war, when groups of Sierra Leonean children were asked what they wanted most for their communities, they said schools. They wanted to learn how to prevent such wars in the future. Who can say no to that?

I visited with Thaimo and Alie, meeting their families over lunch in Alie's home, clay-sided with a metal roof, one of the nicer houses. The women wore dazzlingly colorful dresses and hair wraps, made of what they called country cloth, a kind of thick cotton printed with bright designs, as they brought heaping dishes of food. It was sweltering inside as we shared plates of chicken, fish, and rice. It was also an honor.

Later, waiting outside, looking like a crumpled tissue from riding in a 4x4 and sweating my way through village after village, I asked Fataba what family life is like in Bandankoro. She told me how life is improving, and most children survive and grow to adulthood. Great news! Then she added that older generations, as children, lost many siblings, and sometimes there is in them "a hidden sadness." She looked up at me after smoothing her dress, asking, "Do you understand?" "Yes," I answered, "yes I do."

Review:
Stepping Stones to Help You in Your Loss Journey

Telling your Loss Story out loud is an expression of love for the one you lost and for yourself—and the most important audience is you.

Because we all experience death, telling your Loss Story is a way to build a bridge to other people and to your future life.

By telling your Loss Story, you begin to integrate your loss and harness your grief so it is less likely to ambush you.

In the telling of your Loss Story, you're releasing built up feelings and emotions-—it's a kind of pressure valve to take away some of grief's power to overwhelm you.

2

Losing

What loss looks like

After the storm, some of the trees lie down in mud. Silence takes shape in stunned cows, strewn feathers, sheep wool tangled on wire, and one shingle dropped like a letter in the field, unopened. So much gone. Don't overlook the astonishing fact: you're still here.

— from my notebooks, April 2014

I've come to measure my life in cats. You can't have a lifelong relationship with a cat. Okay, from the cat's perspective often you can. Sometimes I think lucky cat to have the same person cherish and fuss over you your whole life. I'm on my third pair of cats since becoming an adult. Yikes, am I an adult?

Barney and Pumpkin joined me in my early 20s. Barney cat became a true elder, slipping away in his sleep when he was 20½, and Pumpkin made it to age 18. Then came Muir and Maya in my early 40s who each developed intestinal cancer dying at not quite 13 and just past 15 respectively. And now, Tiger and Chloe kittens, technically cats, chase through the house; you can do the math on my age. Is there another pair of cats in my lifetime? Probably not, unless next time around I adopt really old cats.

Perhaps the most poignant aspect of my life at this moment is watching my husband, who, with a failing heart, senses he's likely celebrated his last birthday. He lifts Tiger close to his face, saying, "I'll miss you, little guy." Ironic, of course, because in death you don't miss anyone, they miss you. Dying slowly, over months and years, can leave you grieving the life you're leaving behind. As you lose wellness and abilities, becoming less of who you once were, you literally miss yourself.

I'll miss you. That's what I always think to him when he's nuzzling Tiger like that.

When I talk with others struggling with loss, missing their loved ones is always the hardest part, and there's no real antidote. We also miss ourselves, because we're not the same people anymore. To miss another is to miss yourself, too. But. There are ways to embrace that *missing* and hold the ones we love in new ways, which is part of the journey we're taking together in this book.

Finding Tiger was like Internet kitten dating. My husband and I were both sitting at the local hospital waiting to be called for blood tests when we saw an ad in a newspaper with a pet adoption website. What else can you do when your last cat died two weeks earlier, you're still weepy, and you're waiting to be poked with a needle? Of course, you go kitten shopping on your smartphone.

There were many feline faces and mini-stories to go with each of them. With one flick of a finger, up scrolled a tiny tabby kitten, grey and fluffy, just a couple months old. Then up popped the rest of his litter mates, including one ink-dark girl with brown patches above her eyes, her head tipped sideways looking out of the phone more like an owl than a kitten.

Still mourning our Maya, I didn't think I was ready to adopt. My husband said, "Time is a luxury I don't have."

The ability to love is surprisingly infinite. Loss comes along and breaks your heart, and with the jolt of pain, out pours a stream of possibility. You have the ability to love again and again and again. You just go with the flow, do a bit of paddling through the emotional boulders, and let that stream carry you through loss and back into your life. I'm not telling you it's an easy ride to love and lose and keep loving. But. Know the stream is there, waiting for you to go with it.

What can I say? Before I even met Tiger and Chloe, I was smitten by those kittens.

Look out for loss and value systems.

In talking with others struggling with their losses, two issues almost always come up. Loss is not a one and done experience. It's a Swiss Army Knife with 147 ways to cut. Loss also comes with an unspoken value system, that is, unspoken until someone speaks. Let's tackle the value system first, and since I'm in kitten mode, I have a question for you.

Is it possible to love a cat or a dog or a Senegal parrot more than a person? I don't know about you, but for me, yes, though the only parrot I know is a 30-year-old named Sonny, for a reason. It's not just that some animals are better people than, well, a lot of people. Our animal companions can be key ingredients in the daily routine of our lives.

What happens when they leave us? First, your life can be broken in ways you never imagined possible. Second, human beings can make you feel more isolated in your loss.

One of the strange thorns that come with grief is a usually-hidden, social code around the way to grieve the variety of relationships we lose through death.

After the loss of my step-dog, Gizmo, I was wounded by a woman I worked with in the community. Gizmo was the confident, snaggle-toothed, brown mutt, the size of a grocery bag, who came as a bonus package when I married my husband. Gizmo was my hiking buddy, and even more than 20 years past his death, I can be padding along the beach, come across a rotting gull wing washed up in the sand, and think, *Oh, Gizmo, your nose would go wild with this.* As for the woman, she said she was sorry for my loss "but thank goodness it was just a dog and you can get another one." Yes, she really said that. I'm not a violent person, but that was one of the rare moments when my brain and my hand momentarily conspired to smack a person in the face, but patience and compassion stopped me.

Why do people do that, place their values on your relationships? Loss is not a competition. No loving relationship can be ranked by Likes or measured by the number of stars as if we're all for sale on Amazon.

Some deaths absolutely are more tragic than others. I've worked with several charitable donors who established scholarships to remember a murdered son or daughter. I've heard their loss stories in anguished detail. I've sat at their kitchen table, sometimes with their dog at my feet or cat in my lap. I've cried with them as they recounted the horror of those losses and the often-dramatic turn their lives took in the aftermath.

Maria still has her son's voice on her answering machine more than 20 years after he was mugged and shot leaving a soccer game. He was heading off to college when he recorded the outgoing message so callers would think there was a man in the house and not his divorced mother living alone. Maria admitted her life was stuck in disbelief that he's never coming home, her grief evolving into a perpetual depression. When I asked if she was getting support, she answered calmly, "I don't want to be happy," acknowledging the choice she'd made. When she misses her son, she listens to his voice on the little cassette tape. Worried that it would break, she found a friend who could copy the message to her computer, then eventually, moving into the cellular age, as a music file on her mobile phone.

Alan and Cindy's daughter was assaulted and stabbed by a group of teens she'd been trying to help. They shared heart-wrenching stories of sitting in court listening to the details of her death. Looking into the face of the oldest one who'd taken their daughter's life, they couldn't make sense of his matter-of-fact tone as he testified. Feeling alone and unsupported, when the trials were over, they sold their home and spent five years traveling the country in a mobile home reaching out to support other parents facing the fresh loss of a murdered child.

Loss is like clay. You can shape it, choose how much power it will have in your life, and decide what that power looks like. If death has just visited you, it may be too soon to consider this idea. When you're ready, ask yourself: What if I thought about my loss like clay? I know it's not easy to think, let alone act that way, but what if?

Let me tell you about another of my donors, Greta. Greta was financially comfortable but not wealthy. She wanted to create a memorial to her friend who passed away suddenly in her sleep, but she struggled fiercely with guilt. Why? Her daughter told her she should be doing the memorial to her husband who died in an accident years earlier. Greta couldn't afford to do two memorials, and for whatever reason, a memorial to both of them didn't seem quite right.

"I think I am a bad wife," she said, with a wobbly voice. "I loved my husband, though you know, he traveled a lot. It was a terrible accident that took him, not a good death." She paused, staring past me at the wall, and I could see the accident replaying inside her. "I know we're supposed to love our husbands above all, except God, and I do. But my friend, she and I talked every day. We were on the phone if we didn't see each other, just checking in, telling each other what birds came to our feeders. We shared tomatoes and zucchinis and cut flowers from our gardens. She was just how I got through some days."

This is what you need to understand that no one told me, that I had to figure out on my own. There's a difference between the facts of someone's death and the impact of their life in your life.

Greta's daughter wasn't helpful in placing her values on her mother's relationships and grief. Unfortunately, the people who love us as well as those who don't really know us, often judge us. Both losses, husband and friend, changed Greta's life in unwished-for ways.

Understandably, Greta's daughter was only feeling the grief of losing her father, so she couldn't understand her mother's grief for her friend. But. The loss of Greta's friend, while not tragic in how her death happened, disrupted Greta's life more than the loss of her husband because her friend was a part of each and every day. With her husband traveling frequently, she'd already learned to live without his physical presence in her daily life. Greta's sorrow for both her friend and her husband was made so much worse because of a social value system.

There's a daily-ness to losing your person.

Sometimes even the grief support professionals miss this point. The daily-ness of a relationship, severed by death, has a lot to do with how devastated we feel. We're not supposed to say out loud that we grieve more for a close friend than a spouse or someone who died peacefully more than the one tragically taken or even a pet more than a human, but it happens. It's normal.

In working with Greta to create a memorial, she asked what I thought. Name it for her friend or her husband? I'm wise enough not to step into someone else's loss-tinged decision. I just asked a two-part question. "What do you really want to do, and do you think your husband and friend would understand?" She was silent and took a sip of tea from her cup. "They would both understand either way." After another sip, nodding to herself, "My husband knew how close I was to her."

If we are to be real in confronting loss, let's acknowledge that losing those we love who were part of our daily life and routines is going to be an especially challenging journey. We'll talk about this concept later. For now, just know that without addressing the many daily losses that come with the death of someone you love, your ability to move forward with your life may be blocked.

Honestly, the loss of my cat companion, Muir, remains one of the hardest losses for two reasons. First, the moments before he left us were grim to witness. Second, and more profoundly, Muir was a part of so many hours of every day for almost 13 years. This is why the death of an animal companion can be so hard if you are an "animal person," especially if the humans in your circle of friends and family are not.

Muir was white with grey tiger-patches, including one shaped like a lopsided heart, and he had a long, striped, expressive tail. Every morning he sat on the bathroom counter watching me wash my face and brush my teeth, studying me like a researcher, rotating his ears and blinking, trying to make sense of human behavior. We had little routines together. When I'd bend forward and flip my hair towards the floor to brush it from the underside, he'd crawl under the waterfall of my brown and grey strands, roll onto his back, and look up to me, then I'd brush his snowy belly.

Other times when I was hustling through the house with my head full of thoughts or running late or trying to get through chores, he'd wait to the side of a doorframe, and when I came barreling out of a room, he'd jump as high as he could, kicking off the wall, doing a kind of gymnastic half-twist or somersault. When he landed back on the floor, he'd turn and look up at me as if to say, *What did you think of that? Now pay attention.* I couldn't help but stop, smile, and celebrate Muir's performance. It not only entertained me, but it got me out of my mindless rushing and mindfully back into the moment.

The last morning of Muir's life, my husband and I nestled him between us in bed, along with our other cat, Maya, gently stroking his fur, talking quietly and telling Muir stories to celebrate his feats and his love. A few hours later, there was a brief but awful moment of disbelief as my husband and I, and Maya, too, realized that was it. Muir struggled to breathe. I wrapped him snug in a blanket like a newborn and placed him in my husband's arms. They looked at each other, and then he left us.

Loss is the Swiss Army knife you never wanted.

Let's talk about the Swiss Army knife-like nature of loss. Loss can cut in so many not so handy-dandy ways. First, on a fundamental level, there are so many types of loss. There is the obvious one we're talking about here: the one you love is gone or leaving soon on their end-of-life journey.

Are there other kinds of losses? Yes! Marriages end. Children are consumed by addiction. Careers shift. Breasts get cancer and have to be removed. The childhood home is now an airport runway. Memories seep away. Chronic illness and aging change abilities. Violence rages against people of color, played again and again in the streets and on the television.

Losses often hit us all at once. In the last several months, as my husband's health declined, it's seemed our world was simply falling apart. The Prius' nifty hybrid battery died. The 18-year-old mesh deck chairs suddenly ripped, one after another, my bottom surprised each time. A facia board along the roofline of my home office crumbled at the touch of a hand, rot hidden beneath the paint. A hearty Himalayan rhododendron that's endured for years is now a collapsed withered presence, it's big, waxy, oval leaves, drooped and yellowing. Almost every day something has snapped, shattered, or sputtered to a stop. Do you know what I mean?

Let's also toss in a pandemic. In this moment as I write, everyone on this planet is feeling a range of losses or some sense of grief thanks to the invisible, uncontained spread of COVID-19. Who misses freedom and the ease of leaving the house for dinner with friends, the sight of a face without a mask, or an everyday hug? Out of habit, I still slide on lipstick before jumping in the now repaired car only to realize it will end up smeared inside my favorite dragonfly mask. Who knew I'd ever have a favorite face mask?

A donor I knew, originally from Sri Lanka, once told me that when your world is falling apart, it's because you need to be distracted while the heavenly creator is planning something wonderful for you. Well, there must be a dazzling, incredible, phenomenal future just around the corner. What do you think?

One loss is many losses.

Part of the confounding nature of loss is what I call its gopher effect. Have you ever looked out at your yard or city park and seen mounds of fresh dirt? Below the surface, those big-toothed, persistent rodents will tunnel through your landscape and pop up uninvited in both unpredictable and very predictable places. I've seen a pansy, its purple-yellow flower delicate as tissue paper, suddenly start vibrating, and watched as the stem, leaves, and blossom were slowly sucked into the ground, disappearing. Sometimes after such a magic trick, the gopher will poke his furry face out of the hole, ever so briefly, part in curiosity and part in triumph.

Loss is something of a gopher in our lives. It's with you all the time, working below the surface, making itself known on its own schedule. Any attempt to route it out of your garden of grief and survival is limited, because at some point and then another and then another, loss will demand attention. Without a life-support system for working through loss, it can suck your fragile happiness down into a familiar dark hole.

One afternoon I ran into a neighbor, the two of us walking our one-lane road, socially distanced in this pandemic of course. She lost her husband about 16 months earlier, a kind, community-spirited man who didn't deserve the neurological disease that mangled his body in the three years before his death. Before we even said hello and how's COVID treating you these days, she blurted, "What are you supposed to do about birthdays and anniversaries?" Good question.

Every year specific dates are tied to love and loss. You not only have their birthday, now you have their death day, too.

Besides family- and faith-oriented holidays and the traditions that go with them, there are the milestones. There are wedding days, graduation days, First Communions or Bat Mitzvahs, the day she gave birth, the day he headed off to boot camp, retirement day, the day you summited the mountain together, the day you saw each other across the room, even the day you both lost someone else you loved and comforted each other.

For one donor that I used to work with, it was a day of the week, rather than a date, that initially haunted her, Tuesdays. During the near decade her husband, as she put it, "tangoed with cancer," there was always some sort of treatment or appointment on Tuesday. Her husband would be drained, no appetite, so she'd swing by one of the Mexican restaurants for a Taco Tuesday to-go order for her dinner. I asked her if she still likes tacos, and surprise, she said yes. While Tuesdays were tough, the tacos still remind her of her husband, how they faced his illness together, and the way he kept his sense of humor through it all. "He called me his crunchy wife," she said, grinning, "and I can still be her."

There are all the big days you shared in the past, then all the big days in the future you won't get to share. Loss has its seasons. As the calendar moves through its cycles, you'll miss the one you love often, almost on schedule, especially in the first year or two. Each person we lose is so many losses in one—that's another Swiss Army Knife-like feature of loss.

We need to build our own, unique Emotional Flak Jacket to get us through now and to spring into action when the gopher of loss pokes his head up in the future. Ideally, we should identify the meaningful dates and days before we're there. For some of us, hanging on to old traditions, maybe even setting a plate at the holiday dinner table as some do, will be the best way to move forward and still hold on to the ones we've loved and lost. For others, those traditions will never feel right again, and an empty plate at the table would throw the day or the week into despair.

Fortunately, we are a creative species, and we can design and develop new traditions that bridge our former lives with our survivor selves.

Another of my donor acquaintances heads out to the beach every Christmas Day, first thing in the morning, where she talks to her long-gone and deeply adored daughter for a few minutes, sings "Here Comes Santa Claus" to the sea, then leaves a small feast of crab legs for the gulls. Her husband calls it a waste of good crab. Why does she do it? "If I can't make Christmas breakfast for Sara, I'll make it for the gulls she loved to chase as a child."

Whether your first year or the second or the tenth after your loss will be most difficult is unique to each person and each loss. For some, getting through the first year means every holiday or anniversary is like a bomb. For others, the first year passes in such a blur of numbing transition, it's the second year that's a minefield. All I can say is when you are having a pretty good moment, try to envision the critical dates and days you'll inevitably miss the one you love. Then plan for revising old or creating new rituals or traditions to soften and minimize the pain that will pop up.

Don't put it off, and don't get stuck in "I don't know how I'll handle that day" and just let it hit you like a tsunami. Somewhere between an empty plate and crab legs for seagulls, there's a way to maneuver through those special days emotionally, mentally, physically, and spiritually intact. Later we'll talk about Tiny-Come-Back-to-Your-Senses Rituals and Joy Habits, which can be helpful practices as part of that maneuvering.

There are a few other dates to plan for that can cause trouble in the midst of your loss and potentially magnify the depth of your grief.

For most of us born in the last millennium, 9/11 remains a sensitive date—a day of deep personal loss for many families and a communal loss for the rest of us. If you lived through World War II, then you also have December 7th, Pearl Harbor Day, as another solemn time. Those dates are layered with loss. A sense of being safe or secure was taken from us. We also lost the comforting illusion, at least for awhile, that death is far away. We saw how individuals went from breakfast to grave in an instant and realized the next time it could be us. Anyone alive and old enough to remember those dates knows exactly what they were doing and how they felt when the brutal news reached them.

Ironically, on September 11, 2001, part of my memory is waking up on the rug after sleeping on the floor with my tortoiseshell cat, Pumpkin, tending to her all night after what would turn out to be an unsuccessful surgery to remove cancer from her mouth. Her plump body grown thin, half of her face swollen and bandaged, she didn't move when I got up. After making a cup of tea, bleary-eyed, I turned on the television just after the first plane hit the first tower. Flame, smoke, chaos. I was living in Pennsylvania then, so the experience was in real time. In stunned confusion, I glanced down at Pumpkin, a limp purse of fur. When I looked back up, the second plane slammed into the second tower. Bits of debris fell from the buildings, some of which turned out to be people, then each massive tower collapsed.

Did you feel as powerless that day as I did? September 11th will always bear the enormous loss of human lives compounded by the remembrance of my little cat's suffering and passing.

Death was unfolding all around me. Yet, as I stepped out onto the deck, it was the most beautiful, quiet fall morning. The sky was a deep, endless blue ocean above me, cloudless, dew glistened on ferns and leaves, and goldfinches, yellow as sun, partied at the birdfeeder as if nothing unusual was happening.

How can ugliness and beauty coexist in the same moment?

Eventually I learned to reframe that question into a statement: Ugliness and beauty coexist in every moment.

Those words remind me that in the midst of grief there is also joy. Sometimes you have a little work to do to bring the joy to into your life—that's what I want to help you do through this book. Please know joy is there with you, maybe you can't feel it yet, but it really is there.

Review:

Stepping Stones to Help You in Your Loss Journey

Though loss comes along and breaks your heart, it also opens new (if initially unwelcome) possibilities, including an ability to love in so many ways.

There's a difference between the facts of someone's death and the impact of their life in your life. Grief and mourning will usually be more challenging when a loved one played a large role in your day-to-day life.

Unspoken value systems can complicate your loss. People around you may view certain kinds of losses as more life-altering or grief-worthy than others. Loss is not a competition. Only you know the true depth and dimensions of your loss.

Other people will sometimes say stupid things. The vast majority of the time, they mean well. Let go of the of hurtful words and forgive them—you don't need to carry the extra weight of anger and disappoint.

Loss comes in many forms, beyond the death of a loved one, and can magnify your grief. By being aware of these other losses and tending to them, you'll have more stamina to your grief.

Loss has its own seasons. Loss pops up on key dates, specific days, holidays, and milestones. By deciding well in advance how you will modify traditions or create new rituals, you'll limit the depth and duration of the darker grief emotions.

 There's no antidote to missing the one you love. However, just as ugliness and beauty coexist in every moment, you can cultivate joy alongside the longing and hold that relationship in a new way in your life.

3

Grieving

The kaleidoscope of grief

The whole body is a prayer. Beyond hands and mouth, beneath the soft armor of flesh, the hidden channels of blood pulse their pleas. The heart can't speak, so the language is pain, asking, Please and Why, over and over.

— from my notebooks, May 2003

A bobcat in the rain! It's rare to see a bobcat, let alone in the clouded daylight of a May morning sitting on an open hill. A light, balmy rain was falling on her lovely bobcat body. Grabbing my binoculars for a closer look, she was covered in diamonds, droplets of water clinging to the tips of her fur making her star-studded and glittery.

Have you ever seen a bobcat? They are night-lovers. Bigger than a cat, they have a striped face and leopard-ish spots mottling their bodies, which are a bit chunkier, their legs proportionally shorter, than a couch kitty. Their most defining feature? A bobcat's tail is short, thick, and fluffy, more like a jack rabbit's, whom a bobcat would gladly invite to dinner, as dinner.

This one, between my house and Ruth's, my neighbor and friend, was a living statue. Enduring the steady downfall, she rarely blinked until a bead of water dripped down from whisker-like tufts above her eyes. As I gingerly stepped out on the deck to be in the morning with her, my husband phoned Ruth to grab her binoculars. Ruth loved animals, too. We always alerted each other to birds, bears, foxes, and the return of monarch butterflies—whatever came fluttering or trotting through our shared landscape.

Bobcat spent the morning in that spot before disappearing into the woods. I hoped the magical sighting would lift Ruth's spirits. Laid off not long after enduring cancer and radical surgery, along with some health system politics as a medical professional, she hadn't been her quirky, funny self for a while. It rained all day and night and into the next morning.

Surprise, Bobcat was back, apparently happy to be rained on and just looking around, as if wondering, *so this is what daytime is like*. Again, we called Ruth, picking up a bleakness in her voice. When the rain cleared, Bobcat was back off into the maples and hemlocks. I'd planned to step out on the deck that night to see if Bobcat might be there, but didn't. Instead, we were awakened at nearly 1:30 in the morning by a local sheriff. As my husband stumbled out to the front door, sleepy and muttering about the hour, I don't know why, but I immediately thought, *Ruth. Something's wrong.*

The sheriff asked if we'd heard any shots. "No." Anything unusual in the neighborhood. "No." (Bobcat was our secret.) Then he left. Going to the kitchen window, we could see police cars and lights at Ruth's house. We slept restlessly and in the morning called Ruth, getting only an answering machine.

I waited for Bobcat to return, but the hill between our house and Ruth's was empty. Later that day her husband called. Ruth shot herself in the heart, apparently under the tree that my kitchen window looked out upon.

Stunned, I sobbed until I was sick. Why didn't I step out on the deck that night? Maybe I would have seen her, could have stopped her. We heard her sadness through the phone. Why didn't I run up the hill to her and hug her or tell her something silly?

Ruth, my husband, and I shared a love for being tricksters. We used to put on wild masks—a werewolf for my husband or me, Ruth's more of a monster face. We'd take turns popping up in each other's window for a good startle and laugh. Once she placed two, palm-sized velvet bears with bobbing heads on our deck, then called us frantically to say, "Quick, look out your window, your deck is being taken over by bears!" When one odd-bird person finds another it's a kind of heaven.

Have you ever lost someone to suicide? My mind cycled like a trapped odd-bird: Why didn't I do this or do that? It's what you do—you run a million scenarios in your head about what you could have, should have done, and how it's too late. It's forever, too late.

My other reflex when the world boggles my mind is to try to learn everything about whatever it is. It was still the early days of the Internet. Yahoo was the go-to search engine, and Google wasn't yet a verb. Even back then, so much came up when I searched on *suicide* and *why suicide*.

Curious facts I now know: Twice as many people die from suicide than murder. So the person who poses the greatest threat to you is apparently you. Also, the sheer presence of a gun in the house raises the likelihood that that someone in that house will turn it on themselves. Damn.

Are you should-ing on yourself?

Suicide is an extreme case, but in reality, losing anyone you love will turn you into a caged bird to some degree, emotionally pacing the variety of rarely real and mostly imagined ways in which you are a dreadful human being who could have, should have saved someone. You'll ask "Why?" over and over, and there will only be silence.

Another surprise—you might not even realize how much you love and care about a person until they're gone. Ruth's death devastated me in ways that I never could have predicted. At times in those early days and weeks, I could not stop crying, in that deep belly-hurting, stabbing-headache way. Friends and colleagues said things like, "I didn't realize you were that close to her." And I'd say, "Neither did I," and that was the rub.

If I can help you with one thing right now, it is this: You can never know a person fully.

As much as you think you know someone, you'll discover in disconcerting ways they were a stranger to you. Even couples married 60 or 70 years can be surprised when their beloved dies and they realize there's so much they didn't know about the person they knew best.

I recall one elder I worked with in his mid-90s still living in the home he'd bought for his new wife and baby, with money borrowed from his father, before heading off to serve in World War II. When I met him, he'd just lost his wife, his high school sweetheart. Going through her things, he was stunned by what he found. She'd been an immigrant who came to the U.S. as a girl with nothing, so she saved everything.

Sweet and lengthy letters to her sister, who'd died long before she wrote them, popped up in odd places. *What was that about?* he wondered. There were notebooks full of poems and big envelopes with illustrated stories she must have created for their children. Apparently, she loved to write. There were three yellowed, fire-singed report cards with glowing teacher notes. "My God," he said, "she could have been a scientist. And what fire happened to her? She never spoke of it." Then a revelation. "Her favorite color was green. I always thought it was blue. Look at all the blue in this house. Now I realize," he whispered, mostly to himself, "blue is my favorite color, all this blue she brought into our life was for me."

How could I know the true burden of Ruth's losses—job, health, sense of self, and what else? While we weren't best friends, she was my kindred, cat-person friend, and we cat-sat for each other whenever trips came up. Ruth loved scuba diving, never missed a television episode of *Survivor*, described herself as a recovering Catholic who'd been ruler-smacked by too many nuns, and couldn't help buying up the imperfect apples every fall to slice and toss out for the young deer heading into their first Pennsylvania winter. She'd call to my husband and me on the deck as we watched her with the apples. "I know, I know, you're not supposed to feed the wildlife, but I also know you'll be watching them just the same." She was right.

Yes, Ruth and I certainly felt we knew each other, until she died, and I discovered she carried a deep mystery that I'd never be able to explore or understand.

You always grieve at least two, and usually three deaths.

Have you already discovered that each death involves grieving multiple deaths? There's your person, there's you, and there's your shared relationship. It was obvious to me for the first time with Ruth's departure. She was about my age, just one year younger, so the specter of my someday death popped up as startling as Ruth in her monster mask sneaking up to our backdoor. She was just 42. The entirety of her life, all that she was, everything she could ever be or become, was done, over. Poof. Her life seemed more like 42 seconds.

Mortality. We avoid thinking about it until we see it in someone else.

The death of those we love can serve as a mirror to our own tentative lives. Grieving Ruth, I grieved for me, reminded that the clock was ticking away on my life. Grieving your own death might not happen at a conscious level. Instead, it may operate below the surface, leaving you with a vague sense of fear or anxiety that you don't understand.

With Ruth gone, my mortality became more real. Had I lived well enough, done my best, treated others as kindly as I could, lived up to my full potential, made a difference in the world? It's easy to beat up on yourself, to look at your flaws and imperfections instead of what you've given and the meaningful ways you've no doubt touched others. Then, if you're like me, you feel guilty for even reflecting on your own life, when, hello, this person who was important in your life just died. What kind of selfish witch are you?

It took a conversation with my mother, who would die only two weeks later, though I didn't know that then, to realize I couldn't have saved Ruth from whatever dark despair led her to her decision.

Grief looks like more than sadness.

Fast forward several years. I was sharing dinner with one of my favorite donors, an artist who said the only reason she could give to charity is that her mother divorced well and then left it all to her. Catching up with each other, she plopped her fork down with a thud in the middle of the table. Matter-of-factly she said, "I threw a hot burrito at the back of my husband's head last night. What the hell? What's wrong with me?" She described an irritating conversation, but nothing worthy of pummeling one's husband with a hot burrito.

Her mother had been gone about three years at that point. "I'm so passed grief," she assured me. Then she shared some other behaviors that puzzled her. A three-dimensional artist who worked mostly in clay, suddenly she couldn't make people, human forms, her sculptures emerging as twisted, unrecognizable shapes. Also, she wanted to eat all the time. She poked herself in the belly, joking, "If this were a baby, I'd be delivering a bouncy baby bowl of pasta."

This is what grief looks like, at least for a wry artist. What does your grief look like?

We think of grief as tears and sadness, maybe with a side of isolation and bouts of numbness. In reality, grief spans every emotion and behavior, and is unique to each individual. It can come and go like a tornado, especially if you haven't given it the attention it begs for.

My artist-donor, for instance, said she didn't want to "wallow" in tears and "self-pity" (her phrases) in the immediate months after she lost her mother to a two-year struggle with metastatic breast cancer. She threw herself into her art, kept busy with family, and did community work. She'd been doing "just fine, thank you very much" until the last few months.

I asked her, "Can you describe what you are feeling?" She scrunched her eyebrows, thinking, and said, "I'm a giant craving full of rage."

We laughed. We also acknowledged how accurately, symbolically, those words described grief. Craving, simply defined, is a powerful desire, yearning, or longing for something or someone. And rage? Rage and anger are the stepsisters of grief. "You think I'm just pissed off that cancer took my mom away?" "Maybe," I answered, "and more."

Cancer. Mom. Death. As we explored in the last chapter, there are a multitude of losses that unfold with each death. Similarly, there are diverse expressions of grief that emerge from that one moment when you go from having a mother to being motherless.

Grief is multifaceted.

Children are kaleidoscopes of unexpected emotions as they try to comprehend death and journey through the new territory of grief. When my sisters died, my mother made it clear to my father and me that we wouldn't ever speak of the fire or the girls. That's hard for a little kid.

Beyond my imaginary friend who lived with me for a good five to six years and was such a wonderful ally, I did some weird stuff. I made up fantastical worlds and alternate truths. I told a second-grade teacher I was really from China and my father was a spy-astronaut. I wove a tale to a classmate that I was a Jewish princess in hiding. In all fairness, my father had traveled for weeks at a time for work in Taiwan, and I missed him. Then he'd landed a contract job with NASA developing cameras for rockets before we sent men to the moon. So maybe I wasn't all that creative.

For several weeks, though, when we lived in a certain trailer park, I took a broom stick without the broom part and pretended it was a crutch for my permanently broken leg. One of my chores was to take the garbage out to the dumpster. After stepping out of the trailer, I'd grab my broomless stick and hobble off limping and wincing as if hurt. Every day an elderly neighbor, almost hobbling himself, would come to my rescue, helping me toss my bag of trash. He doted on me, and I loved it, at least until he approached my mother about taking our garbage for us because he wanted to help the poor little girl. Jig was up on that one. My mother was furious, "You little liar, what's wrong with you?"

If I could have answered as the adult I am now, I would have said, "Grief, Mama, grief with no outlet is what's wrong with me." Actually, even in the throes of grief, there's nothing really wrong with you. You're just you, flailing about in the alternate truth of being a survivor, living in a world that can feel fantastical in not-so-great ways.

Even our animal companions grieve in their own animal mode. The afternoon following the death of Muir cat, our surviving cat, Maya, a gentle calico, did something I'd never seen her do previously or afterward.

Before I could stop her, Maya dug up a baby gopher and shook it by the neck with her teeth, a few quick snaps, until it was dead. Then she walked around the yard tossing it with her mouth up into the air like a bean bag, flinging it as far as she could swing her head, retrieving it, and flinging it up and away again. Horrified, my first instinct was to take the poor, soft, lifeless pouch of gopher from her, but decided, since it was already gone, to let her do whatever it was she clearly needed to do. She kept up the grisly gopher flinging for nearly an hour, then watched me bury it, the second burial of the day.

Twisted clay, nonsensical lies, gopher flinging—if you think like my craving, raging artist, "I'm so past grief," think again.

Over the years getting to know a lot of individuals, hearing their loss stories, talking about grief and healing, I've seen how grief is a chameleon, able to change its colors, adapting to different environments. Grief can look like: eating all the time or skipping meals, literally crying over spilt milk or inexplicably laughing at a funeral, hanging out at a bar with the gang every night or hiding head-down in your cubicle when anyone approaches, throwing tantrums or constantly muttering "why bother," and filling every moment with activity or spending the weekend curled, knees to chest, beneath sheets.

More than emotional or behavioral, grief can look like physical issues: autoimmune flares, attention-deficit disorders, neurological disturbances, chronic fatigue, heart palpitations, carpal tunnel or Achilles tendon ruptures, headaches, gut aches, diarrhea, constipation, burning muscles, and stinging spines. Ten months after my mother died, I developed viral meningitis, and my physician swore it was my grief weakening my immune system that let the virus in. Who knows?

Just know, grief and illness often find each other.

Loss and grief are related but different.

As we talk about loss and grief, let's make sure we're on the same page. Rather than a clinical definition, let me share how I've come to understand the difference between loss and grief.

Loss is the fact and moment when someone or something playing a meaningful role in your life is taken away. Here we're talking about the death of someone you love, but it could be the loss of a partner to divorce or an ovary to disease or a home to a wildfire. I think of loss like a wound—there's what causes the wound and the wound itself, a hole in your being.

Feelings of loss then are akin to rubbing a finger over the wound, noticing how tender it is, and remembering what happened. Loss is with you every day, forever. Even if the wound visibly heals, what happened to you, what was taken away from you, can never be changed. It is a fact. That's why I say once loss comes along, it comes along with you wherever you go.

Grief, on the other hand, is the range of reactions to the loss. It's the sensation of pain, but as we shared, more than pain. Grief can be emotional, behavioral, mental, physical, and spiritual. Grief does not have to be every day or forever. Yes, you'll experience grief early on and acutely as well as decades later. Grief can be unrelenting for months or years, especially if complicated emotionally, like an untreated infection. It can be a boomerang that you send away until it returns out of the blue, punching you between your shoulder blades.

I know from my own experience and supporting others in their loss journeys that grief can't be ignored or eliminated, but it can be harnessed and integrated into a vibrant life. Some may disagree, but I want you to have this possibility of being able to take the reins of your grief. You can't completely control when grief will visit and how long it will stay, but it is possible to keep grief from consuming you. You can prevent grief from blocking your ability to experience joy and keep you from fully living your "one wild and precious life."

The life support system I've built to help myself live with many losses is proof that we don't have to let grief rule. That system starts with understanding your relationship with loss, grief, and mourning, which we'll explore in the next chapter.

Grief likes odd intersections.

The day after Ruth ended her life, and I scoured the world-wide web as if I could secure the answer to *Why did she do it?*, I found myself typing, *What is the origin of the name Ruth?* Yes, Ruth was her real name. I knew the old Bible story of Ruth yet was still surprised to learn that its Hebrew roots translated as *friend*. There was a secondary Germanic root that conveyed *sorrow*.

Grief looks for meaning, so I thought, *Of course, Ruth was my friend with sorrow.* The word bobcat also took on new meaning for me, that damp wild cat appearing just before she left, now signifying omen as much as wonder.

After a few days of being inconsolable following Ruth's death, I had a risky idea. My mother, dying of small cell lung cancer, had been despairing that being so debilitated by cancer and chemotherapy had turned her into, as she put it, a "useless lump." As long as we are living, even when we're unwell and our lives are growing very small, we still want to feel useful, that we have something to give.

My mother was a fiber artist. Okay, that's not how she described herself, but she had been prolifically quilting, knitting, sewing, embroidering, weaving, and beading incredible works of beauty and inspiration for years.

Being able to create and to lead the new quilters guild she'd just launched with her best friend was out of the question, which greatly magnified her end-of-life depression. At the same time, being the type of mother who listened to her children's woes and gave them nurturing nuggets of wisdom was not her strong suit. She would tell you, as she did me, that she never wanted to be a mother, but it was a role expected of women in her generation, so she did her best, marred by the trauma of our house fire and her own childhood lost to unspoken abuses.

So, my risky idea? What if I gave my mother the opportunity to be that nurturing, wise soul I desperately needed then? What if I carefully poured out my grief and confusion about Ruth and let my mother comfort me?

I know it sounds crazy. It was my job to comfort her, and I'd been doing that as best I could since her diagnosis. I knew the potential of adding to her emotional burden and deepening my own disillusionment and guilt was great. Still, having a mother-daughter moment precipitated by Ruth's inconceivable choice, might help my mother feel "useful." With the cancer blossoming in her body despite the chemo, I knew my mother was ebbing away, so I wanted our remaining time to be a close as possible for both of us.

At that point, I was calling and checking in with her every evening. One evening, as soon as she answered, I started crying into the old, princess-style phone before I could speak my Loss Story about Ruth. My mother was silent on the phone, listening, really listening, which calmed me. Tissue in the other hand, I shared all that had happened. I cried, *Why, Mama, Why?* I exposed my anguish for what I could have and should have done, but didn't, to be there for my neighbor and friend. After 20 minutes or so, I was drained of tears and story and words of regret.

My mother, who rode the rollercoaster of untreated bi-polar disorder my whole childhood and survived a failed suicide attempt, related to Ruth. "Oh, sweetheart," she said, "do you really think bringing her cake and a bouquet or having her for dinner would have changed her mind? No. I can tell you she'd never think, *Oh, this is nice, I guess I won't kill myself after all.*" My mother was blunt and darkly honest.

Suicidal thinking was an area of expertise for her. For the next 20 minutes, she offered insight into the despair that can stalk some people, that haunted her. She assured me that being kind to someone who's desperately sad helps. But if a person feels the need to escape—that was the word she used, escape—then they will find their way. It wasn't about me or anyone else, she said, and thinking I could be anyone's savior is a little narcissistic. She was adamant that someone caught in suicidal depression is in her own silo of tormenting thoughts and feelings.

"You need to save yourself and try to be happy," she urged, "and maybe that gives someone else the courage to keep on going." When she was done, there was still no answer to *Why?*, but I wasn't a terrible person any longer.

My mother also gave me an unexpected gift. For the first time, she permitted me a glimpse into her interior world and introduced me to her private demons. It hurt to know how much she suffered for so many years, but I was grateful.

Before we hung up, she offered one more thought, "So long as you both know you loved each other, when death comes, that's all that matters." Two weeks later, death came to my mother, and it was her very own words that comforted me in her loss. *Oh, Mama,* I thought, *now that's being the ultimate mother.*

Review:
Stepping Stones to Help You in Your Loss Journey

You can never know a person fully. That fact will often surprise you, or haunt you, when someone you love dies. By focusing on what you know and cherishing what you remember about your relationship, it will be easier to let go of self-blame around the potential opportunities you missed to know them better.

You always grieve three deaths, whether or not you realize it. You grieve the person you lost, and reminded of your own mortality, you grieve you. You also grieve the relationship you had with each other.

Grief looks like a million different emotions, behaviors, and impacts, depending on who you are and whom you lost. It's more than sadness or longing, and it affects you on multiple levels: emotional, physical, mental, and spiritual.

Loss and grief are related but different. Loss is a permanent fact: someone you love died. Grief is how you respond to loss.

Grief is not forever or for always. Grief is transient, advancing, and retreating, over days, weeks, months, and years.

Grief looks for meaning, trying to understand the what, why, and how of someone's death. Since death is ultimately incomprehensible, you need to make your own meaning so you can move forward with loss in your life.

It's hard to save other people—sometimes saving yourself inspires others to keep going.

4

Mourning

Mourning is waking up to life again

You released her as ashes a little at a time—into the garden, the slow green river, the swell and surge of the Pacific. Tears every time, their sting, necessary. It took months, though releasing made space. For what? It was joy, that refugee always wanting to come back home.

— from my notebooks, April 2012

Looking out the window, I watched a colorful blur as tall spikes of magenta flowers flashed by. Fireweed. It's one of the first plants to re-inhabit scorched earth after a fire and can persist in unlikely places, like the dry, car-fumed edges of a country road. Whenever I see fireweed, I think, *hope*. It reminds me how the earth always heals and keeps on going.

After my mother's funeral, I rode with my father back to his house. He insisted on driving. He needed to drive, I suppose, to have some measure of control in a life that seemed newly rudderless.

A quiet man who'd married a serious talker, in her absence, his voice found an opening. Memories spilled out of him the whole way home, his storytelling a soft, somber soundtrack to the flaming blossoms swaying on their stalks as we passed.

The loss of two young girls to a house fire and my mother's bi-polar mood swings made for a volatile 47-year marriage. To say we hurt the ones we love the most is an understatement in describing how my mother affected my father. Her words, in moments of anger-fueled depression, could cut to the bone, brutal, and they were aimed at my father more than anyone else.

But in the car that day, there was just 47 years of love. Having said the final goodbye to my mother, my father could only see the vulnerable 18-year-old girl who said she was 23, a dancer he met in a St. Louis bar on his birthday, fell in love with, and ran off to Hernando, Mississippi to marry just three weeks and a day later.

Sometimes it's easier to love the dead than the living. I know that's a terrible thing to say, but it's what I wrote in a notebook around that time. Occasionally, it's just plain true.

In the late stage of COPD (chronic obstructive pulmonary disease, essentially seriously damaged lungs), my father knew his own death was nearing, so no time to waste in bad memories. In fact, not long afterward, he refused to watch any movies or programs that didn't have a happy ending, including the nightly news. "I've seen enough sad endings," he declared, "and life is too short for more."

My father always described himself as a cock-eyed optimist, a line from one of his favorite old musicals. All in our family understood that my mother's cancer, only slowed by chemotherapy, was terminal—even she accepted that—but my father believed she'd bounce back.

As the foreverness of her death sunk in during the months that followed, his grief took on a new dimension. Bitterness. Grief is ever evolving. Like a strange moth moving through its own life cycle, it keeps shape shifting.

With an eight-and-a-half-year age difference, he'd planned their retirement, health care, and modest IRA savings to assure they'd support my mother for a long life as a widow. His bitterness was a mix of anger at a disordered world where an older husband with failing lungs was supposed to die first but didn't, along with frustration that he couldn't change that fact. He began to feel foolish that, in his optimism, he hadn't let himself see his wife was dying.

Most of all, he felt disillusioned. While he focused on the happy in his relationship with my mother, there was a long chain of hurts, endured but unaddressed, that waited just below the surface. They emerged at the end of every day, as he sat alone in a four-bedroom house filled with my mother.

It's healthy not to dwell on the negative . . . to a point. If you don't acknowledge the imperfections that tinge your history with a person, the hard as well as the happy truths of a relationship now disconnected by death, well, you're leaving yourself open to a long fall through a complicated grief abyss.

It took evenings of too much wine and awakening each morning gasping for air and hung over before my father decided it was time to move from grieving to mourning. He used different words, but the same meaning, "Wine only makes the loss worse. Who am I kidding? I miss her, but it was never easy. So, gotta live out whatever time I have left in whatever way I can with these busted lungs."

What is mourning?

Mourning sounds like an old-world activity. Just the word makes many of us visualize a woman spending a year draped in black.

Being a birder, I always have a different connotation. I see Mourning doves. They're plucky iridescent birds that look pink or periwinkle-blue or grey depending on the light. In fact, they're shuffling and cooing outside, scratching the ground for seeds as a write. I love the way their wings whistle when they lift themselves from dirt into air. They don't seem dark or dismal at all. Maybe that's the way to think about mourning—a lift-off, getting your life back into flight.

Mourning is turning your grief inside out. To some that means making your grief public, which is part of the rationale for wearing black in certain traditions, or white in others, for a year or two or life. By letting others know you're a survivor in the process of learning to live without the one you love, they can be more aware. They can give you space to *not* be the you they knew, and ideally, nurturing you on your loss journey.

One of the challenges grievers face today is that they can feel very, very alone. Society doesn't know what to do with loss, grief, and mourning, at least in the developed world. Media celebrates material success, positive thinking, and the belief that diets and science can outwit death. It can seem as if you are a walking accident, everyone looking away, avoiding conversation, as if your community is silently saying, *nothing to see here, keep moving.*

I'm not suggesting the answer to good mourning is wearing black, unless it's a COVID-19 mask. Black face masks are common now. Currently living in pandemic times, the black masks symbolize for me not just protection from an unseen marauder, but also the communal mourning taking place. Millions have died globally, and the life routines we once took for granted have been dismantled.

Going public with your grief, however, doesn't mean you need to shout about it from the top of a mountain. Although, I once did something like that and discovered it feels surprisingly good, releasing a bunch of built-up emotions like a human volcano. You might want to try it.

I stood at the crumbling edge of a Pacific Northwest river and yelled, full-lunged, downstream, "I'm grieving here, people!" Of course, there were no people, and even if there were, my loudest voice was muffled by the louder voice of water as it rushed through stones in our shallow canyon. The only possible audience were Cedar waxwings, zig-zagging across the stream as far as I could see, swallowing up insects that I couldn't. A Cedar waxwing is a bird, a little smaller than a Robin, with a peachy-brown face, grey back, and lemony belly. It's not all that dramatic, until you see the bright yellow edges of its tail feathers and dazzling red wing tips, which make the bird look like it's been dipped in candle wax.

Just seeing those Cedar waxwings, realizing that for a moment I'd taken a break from my grief, was a touch of joy. They didn't stop their fluttering and dining to acknowledge my grief blast, and I remember thinking, *Who says birds are all that different from humans?* Still, it felt good to let my animal body roar.

When I say mourning is turning your grief inside out, it's less about publicly displaying that you are in grief and healing mode. Let me put it this way. Loss happens to you from the outside. Grief happens to you from the inside, as a kind of reflex to the loss. Mourning is something you do, on purpose and with purpose—it ties together your inner and outer selves.

Mourning is about moving from the necessary, though mostly passive, internal experience of grief in all its multifaceted force to a new, active relationship with grief. Mourning is necessary to move from surviving to thriving. Mourning is intentional, a path out of loss limbo. It's the process of harnessing your grief and turning its energy toward the work of adapting to your changed world, shaping a new life, and cultivating joy in your life every day. As a result, the process of growing a new you will be visible externally.

It's good to know what mourning looks like.

I met Etta less than a month after one of her two sons, in his mid-thirties, died in a car accident. Through the charity I was working with, she sponsored two children, one in Kenya and the other in India, which means she donated funds every month so their rural communities could provide education, health care, clean dependable water, sanitation, and essentially a foundation for the families to lift their children out of poverty. She wanted to talk with me because she felt compelled to do "something special" for vulnerable children to honor her son's life, and she needed help figuring out what.

I could see that Etta was well-travelled. As we sat in her living room filled with indigenous artworks, batik wall hangings, and wood carvings of elephants and gazelles, one of the first things she asked was, "Why do people say lost? That they're sorry I lost my son, as if I couldn't keep track of him and he just wandered off?"

How do you respond to a question like that? I just nodded, my eyes staying connected to hers, so she knew I was listening. I gave her space to think through her own question. She told me that when her two sons were still small, she started sponsoring children in the developing world, one child for each son, so that her sons could appreciate "their blessings" and grow into "compassionate men." Etta was divorced, and the way she explained "compassionate men" was her way of saying, not like the abusive man she had to flee from as a young mother.

She had her boys write letters almost every month to their far-away friends, also boys, and received letters back with crayon drawings and occasionally a photo. She pulled out an album with the letters, drawings, and photos of her "other kids" as she thought of them. The first two sponsored boys aged out of the program as young adults at almost the same time each son graduated high school and headed off for a four-year tour of duty in the military. Each son served in different areas of the Middle East, returning home safely to college and careers.

"I sponsor girls now," she shared, "because I always wanted a daughter, but never wanted to get married again." Etta had raised her sons mostly on her own, spending time in a women's shelter, before securing a low-income apartment. The church was key to her life, and she worked at hers part time as she made her way through community college, then "regular college" as she called the university. It took her seven years, but as she pointed out, "I graduated college before they graduated high school!" Her serious face released into a huge smile when she said that.

Studying together at the kitchen table brought her family closer together and made her a role model for the power of education. She'd cleaned the church offices once a month to make the extra money for sponsoring children, because, as she told her boys, they need education to make their lives better, too.

Bachelor's degree in hand, she landed a job in Human Resources at a tech company, eventually finishing an MBA, and moving on to senior roles. She loved to travel, especially to poorer parts of the world, where she felt people may feel forgotten. She'd been to the African continent several times as well as parts of India and South America. She said she was on her own mission to meet people, especially other women with children, and tell them they matter.

When I first met Etta, she was still inconsolable, trying hard come to terms with her son's sudden death. She felt she was failing at work and had taken a leave. She'd spent the two days prior to our visit sitting in her bed staring at a blue wall that seemed to shout *your son is gone*. She joked half-heartedly that she was glad I was there, otherwise she had no reason to shower or get dressed. It seemed cruel to her that her son made it home just fine after surviving road-side bombs and snipers oversees only to have one moment of distraction in a car be fatal.

She was angry with God for taking a son before a mother, and she admitted, for taking her "loving boy" instead of a former husband "who never loved anyone." I could see so many layers to her pain.

Loss is an onion—the more you peel it, the more you find yourself crying. Still, Etta also believed that God was a mysterious presence who had his own reasons, loved her, and expected her to make the most of her life. In my early conversations with Etta, I thought her desire to "do more" philanthropically to help others in the developing world would be a central act in her mourning, and it was.

But over time, what brought Etta back was running. The little girl she sponsored in Kenya had said in a letter that one of her favorite things to do is to run and that she was good at it and that it made her feel "free like a bird." That one line in a letter from a girl she'd never met was a trigger. Etta forgot how, as a young girl, she also liked to run, and couldn't recall why she stopped.

One afternoon, I called her about a well-building project. Before I could say anything, she blurted, "I'm running." In her late 50s, she shared how breathless, out-of-shape, and foolish she felt the first few times she put on an old pair of sneakers and started jogging around her neighborhood. But within a few weeks, she was able to run a couple of miles. She started running as soon as she got up. Her theory was that she had to get going before the grief got going. She'd be so sweaty she'd *have* to take a shower and get dressed. It seemed too simple and silly, yet her theory proved true. She was out of her pajamas, running, and soapy fresh by 7:30 most mornings.

She then set a goal to go visit the girl she sponsored in Kenya and run with her. "I have a lot of running to do before I can do that," she said. After talking about the challenges to building wells in places with little water, and just as we were about to hang up, I quipped, "Have fun with your running." There was a pause, and I thought maybe the call had dropped.

Finally, she said, "It's real. I do feel free like a bird when I'm running." She had created the break she needed from grief and was literally running into a new life.

There's a thread that is your life.

When people ask me how I got into philanthropy, I love to answer, when other little girls wanted to be ballerinas and little boys dreamed of becoming firemen, I wanted to be a charitable gift and end-of-life planner. Of course, no; no one plans to grow up to be "the death and taxes lady," as one of my 80-year-old donors once described me, introducing me to his tribe of retired business friends over lunch.

I don't know why I've landed in philanthropy, not really. And now, I feel this urgent drive to help others work through their loss, grief, mourning, and the very individual process of new-life building in the aftermath of a death. Why?

I believe there is a thread to our lives, and while nothing is predestined, we feel the pull of that thread leading us forward. Even when we're in loss limbo, the way we know we're stuck is because we sense that pull, but we're not moving with it.

We have choices and decisions to make as we exist in this space and time, after all, we are beings with brains and free will. At the same time, we're beings who are part of a larger tapestry of other free wills, and our particular thread has purpose. We're meant to add color, help shape the design, and strengthen the fabric. We influence, and are influenced by, other threads, that is, the other lives around us. We're part of a design that's bigger than our delicate thread. When there's a tear in that tapestry—a death—our thread is ruptured, and the grand design becomes a confusing tangle.

There's a poem, called "The Way It Is," by William Stafford, that's something of a touchstone to me. It talks about this concept. It begins, "There's a thread you follow. It goes among things that change. But it doesn't change." It's a brief but powerful poem that contemplates the range of losses we experience and how we can keep moving forward. The poem is a reminder—despite all that befalls us, there's an essence or a momentum, an invisible thread, at the core of each of our lives. If we stay true to that thread, which is unique to each of us, we can't ever get truly lost in our lives.

Why does my life path look and feel the way it does? Perhaps for me, helping people create meaning out of the tough reality that they are mortal, finite beings or salvage some measure of good out of the heartbreaking losses they've endured, is just my way of holding on to my own invisible thread for dear life.

During the throes of grief, it's easy to let go of the thread, to lose it for awhile. The process of mourning allows you to feel around in the darkness and grab that thread again. There's a drive to weave that thread back into some sense of wholeness, despite the hole.

You can't really define what the thread is. Call it what you will: your core self, your potential, your life force, your spirit or soul, your Buddha nature or luminous mind, The Tao, or the touch of God or the universe within. That thread that runs through your life and wants to keep moving you forward is beyond words, but it's real nevertheless.

For Etta, her thread was that childhood love of running that she rediscovered thanks to a letter from a faraway girl. Funny, when you think about it. Who helps whom? Etta wanted to help a little girl growing up in a poor village have the best life possible. Yet, the little girl helped Etta move toward her own best possible life.

It helps to believe in happy endings.

The sentiment of mutual comforting has been an integral part of my work with people, whether my close loved ones or the wildly diverse range of individuals who have passed through my career.

While you have solo work to do, there's an interdependent element to growing your resilience. Humans are wired to live in relation to other humans, which may simply be family or a few friends or a traditional tribe as I experienced in Sierra Leone or a virtual community of like-minded folk we engage with through social media or web-based Zoom meeting rooms.

As for my father hampered by COPD, running was not part of his good mourning. First, he realized he had unanswered grief from the loss of my sisters. Turns out, he'd always wanted to place a headstone on their grave. Lack of money at the time of the fire and my mother's emotional frailty that didn't allow for conversations about a memorial, had left my sisters' resting place as a numbered plot on a cemetery list and nothing but grass when you found it. Finally, he ordered a headstone in the shape of two hearts to make sure his little girls' long in the earth were, as he put it, no longer anonymous. People will know they were here, and they were loved.

When a family experiences traumatic loss, the individual differences in grieving can destroy marriages and leave some members to suffer in silence and unsupported. We'll explore this side effect of loss later on.

All those years, my father carried such unspoken burden. Still, he was an emotional bootstrapper, as I and my younger sister and much younger brother, who came along well after the fire, would soon discover.

My father reconnected with his thread. As a young man, he dreamed of being a dancer. I never knew that until after my mother, who'd always been the dancer in the family, died. He had old, dusty dreams and stories I never could have imagined until his mourning unearthed them and he spoke them out loud.

So what did he do? He reached out to a family friend of his generation, Lila, a widow who'd been a singer before she married. Spouseless, they were often seated together at family events. He invited Lila to dinner out at a Mexican restaurant then back to the house to watch an old musical together. They made it a weekly habit each Wednesday. "No sex or anything," he told me on the phone. Yikes, Daddy, too much information.

Until my father's death less than three years after my mother's, he and Lila were kindred spirits who, despite their damaged health and losses, found joy every Wednesday night singing and dancing vicariously in a cinematic world with only happy endings.

Review:

Stepping Stones to Help You in Your Loss Journey

Complex relationships may lead to complex grief. Being honest about the relationships you've lost, both the happy and the hard times, will help you better respond to your grief.

Sometimes a roar, literally and physically roaring out your grief, brings some relief.

Mourning helps you integrate loss and grief so you can move forward with your life. Mourning is something you do, on purpose and with purpose. It ties together your inner and outer selves.

Mourning looks as diverse as the people who mourn. A key element of mourning is returning to you-specific activities or habits that cultivate joy in the broken places in your days.

It helps to think of your ever-changing life as moving forward along an invisible thread that never changes. While your life evolves through successes and losses, there is a you who is enduring, resilient, and always moving forward.

5

Becoming

You are a work in progress

You were a tiny thing, a knob of cells. You had the possibility of a tail, and a heart-beat before you grew a heart. The first loss is leaving another's body. Now you are your own universe, a being made of light moving through time. What's next?

— from my notebooks, August 2003

Who do you want to become?

I know it sounds like a question for a child, and it's not grammatically perfect, but it's so much bigger than the familiar what-do-you-want-to-be-when-you-grow-up line.

First, "growing up" is overrated and to me wrong-headed. It suggests there's some end point or destination you reach, as if once you hit 18 or

21 you're done, finished, like bread popping up as toast. Often "growing up" signifies a series of successful losses, as in, losing your sense of wonder, curiosity, belief in unseen possibilities, and confidence to be yourself despite what others around you may want or expect you to be. Let's not grow up, okay?

Second, how you answer the what-do-you-want-to-be-when-you-grow-up question is so culturally dependent. When I was working with a humanitarian organization and traveling to visit project areas with donors, I once asked a little boy in the rural highlands of Ecuador what he wanted to be when he grew up. Stretching his arms above his head, he replied in Spanish, "Alto," meaning tall. Yes, of course.

In America, that when-you-grow-up question almost always means what profession or job do you want to have, such as doctor or teacher or rock star. Ever notice that kids instinctively know the answer is not *unemployed and sleeping in my parents' basement*? That old question is about *what* not *who*. An adult is almost never wondering *who* the interrogated child wants to be, as in thoughtful, motivated, loving, assertive, supportive, collaborative, or just plain happy.

As lifeforms on our little blue planet, we're always in the process of becoming.

Life happens to us. Change is constant, right down to the cells of our body that die and grow anew, all the time, so our physical selves are not the same from one point in time to another.

You are never the same animal twice.

In the 15 or so seconds it took me to write that line, about 15 million of my cells died. Miracle, I'm still here, because new cells were also born. I'm a literally different person, yet there's this thread of sameness, this immutable self that I can lose and come back to.

Even after one is clinically deceased, it takes hours for all cells to die and relinquish their genetic drive to keep becoming the next version of themselves. With the body's defenses gone, some cancer cells even become more active for awhile after death. Their bias for rebirth is not easily defeated.

What is becoming?

Of course, you and I are not just physical sacks of cells. We are emotional, psychological, and spiritual beings tied to these organic bodies of ours. So, we're always *becoming* on multiple levels.

The concept of becoming means everything is impermanent, in flux. There's an ever-present possibility for evolution, renewal, and growth as an individual. Change is happening around us all the time, whether we realize it or not, and we are constantly responding to those changes. In the process, we are altering who we are from moment to moment.

It's easy to see the physical shifts as the body passes through time, becoming older. Notice any new wrinkles lately? The emotional and psychological transitions are less apparent. I won't even try to address spiritual transformation.

Over time the effect of many tiny adaptations as we become this, then this, then this, can be dramatic. Anyone who's ever had a collapsing relationship or divorce can attest to how much they and their partner "became different people." Not only is your sweetheart not who you thought they were, they are not who they thought they were.

Most of the time we're not thinking about who we are becoming, let alone how death intercepts that process.

Eighteen months after my mother died, sitting in a house by a river on the other side of the country from where I left her, it hit me. I'd become motherless. On one hand, it's obvious, a fact. But. The impact of being motherless had quietly altered the course of my life. My mother was the one person on the planet who had truly known me my entire life, right down to being an eyeless, almost-heartbeat with a tail, an embryo, inside her.

Identity includes our relationship to others.

Without a mother, what did it mean to be my mother's daughter? My role as her daughter didn't exist anymore. I was still my father's daughter, but I realized that was a different role. Similarly, what did it mean to be Ruth's friend and neighbor without Ruth? When my father died sometime later, I became an orphan. If we outlive our parents, we all become orphans.

Part of defining who you are is how you exist in relationship to other people. When loss comes along, you lose roles, parts of your identity. It's not always a bad thing. Sometimes there's a kind of freedom.

While I still want to live up to my mother's highest expectations for being a "good girl" and thus a good woman, I've been pleasantly surprised in the years since her death to be giving myself permission to do things and move through the world in ways that somehow seemed off-limits when she was still on this planet. I can't tell you why that would be, only that it is. No, I haven't turned into a selfish brat, I just intuitively discovered I can be a kind human in more ways than my mother defined.

Thinking about your loss, what roles have changed or simply gone away for you?

Besides daughter, mother, friend, and the usual relationship titles, there are other roles that describe us and are tied to our loved ones. Think: traveler, business partner, soccer coach, home schooler, hiker, hunter, Phillies fan, and what else? Who else have you been, and are you still that person now?

One woman whom I met working for an Alaska-based organization told me she lost a third of herself when her husband died. Kayaking was a big part of their lives. Once the days got long heading into summer, they paddled the chilly bays of Southeast Alaska until fall made it too dangerous—so about a third of their year was spent on water, together. It could be rainy and waves choppy, but they were rewarded with views of huge snowy peaks appearing between clouds, harbor seals swimming under their kayaks, and up-close encounters with retreating glaciers.

When her husband died suddenly of an embolism, she lost her role as both wife and kayaker. We talked about the potential of kayaking with a friend, but she assured me it would never be the same. I lost contact with her, but later heard she was living in the lower 48 and had horses. No longer a kayaker, she became a horsewoman. *Perfect solution*, I thought, *wild mane and hooves plowing currents of air rather than water, and a new companion in the form of a horse.*

As you process your loss, it helps to recognize the roles you played when your loved one was with you. You are more than your roles, yet it's pretty difficult to know who you are without some roles connected to the people you care about. You can't answer who you want to become if you don't know who you've been, yes?

Moving forward is fact, how you do it is a choice.

I can't think of any change that's more dramatic and severe than the death of someone you love. Have you considered the possibility, though, that the process of moving forward from your loss presents the opportunity to become a version of you that's more than just different or damaged?

While this new you may not be anything you ever imagined, or asked for, what if you can shape a life after loss that is utterly beautiful? I'm not suggesting there's some silver lining to loss or trying to tell you to look on the bright side of it all. Nor am I saying, *hey, just move on*, as many around you may be advising, meaning, get over your loss. Yikes! No.

The fact is, if you are alive, the days are coming and going so you are literally moving forward in your life, even on those days you feel stuck and completely immobile in a grief hole. You are becoming someone else because your invisible thread stretches through time and constant change, including bouts of chaos and calm along the way.

While a death can feel like time has stopped, you also know that troubling truth: the world keeps on going anyway. Around you people are still buying groceries, watching basketball or going for a run, chatting it up on their smartphones, bundling up their kids for a ride on a sled, and playing frisbee with their dogs. You've seen them laughing and walking about as if nothing happened. The hands of time only move in one direction—forward, into the future of the next moment and the next and the next. No, time hasn't stopped for your loss.

What I'm saying is, you might as well grab that invisible thread, hold it like reins, and choose where the pony goes. You won't be in control all of the time, because as you know too well, some things really are out of your control.

Feeling overwhelmed, lost, anxious, numb, and the diverse expressions of pain will cloud your view and you'll lose your grip at times. But. If you set an intention about *who* you want to become in the aftermath of your loss, your invisible thread can also function as a lifeline. When grief with all its tentacles of emotion comes for a visit, you'll be better able to be with it, to move through it or let it move through you, and to pull your pony hooves out of the mud and slog onward.

After two long years lost in grief's netherworld following my mother's death, knotted perpetually to Ruth's suicide, when I finally focused with intention on *who* I could become, I surprised me. Following those losses, I'd moved across the continent to accept and ultimately leave an executive position that turned out to be a terrible fit, even if I hadn't been dancing with the darkest feelings of loss. My first instinct was to define what I wanted in my career, asking, *What do I want to do?* I realized quickly, however, you can't figure out your work aspirations until you seriously wonder— *Who do I want to become?*

How did I surprise me? I stopped thinking about career success and job titles, and I focused on my obituary. I didn't actually write an obituary, but I did draft an epitaph, that final, engraved statement that goes on a headstone. It dawned on me that if I were reading my obituary and epitaph, I wouldn't want it to dwell on what I did for a living, though my work in philanthropy is part of me. I'd want that line or two summarizing my time on the planet to express what *kind* of person I was.

When you condense the entirety of your life to a blurb and a photo, what do you want it to say?

Media mogul Ted Turner once famously quipped that he didn't want his tombstone to read, "I never owned a network." Having launched CNN, he doesn't have to worry about that, but defining one's self in material terms is not *Who* anyone is as a human being. We never really own anything in this world, whether a home or a bowl of fruit. We're temporary caretakers. Someone else will eventually live in this room in which I now write. My kittens sleeping by the window and I will disappear into history. I'll eat the bowl of fruit, it will become me, and together we return to the earth.

What you need to consider is this: *Who* you are affects others, and they affect others. Your impact is bigger than you. *Who* you choose to become matters, and *becoming* is a process that is never finished until you are. Even when the physical *you* is gone, your *Who* continues. We're each that well-known drop in the pond that's forever rippling through the water.

When you define *Who* you want to become, clearly and succinctly, you are describing the essence of your invisible thread, your soul or spirit or life force within you, that doesn't change even as the facts of your day-to-day and decade-to-decade life are always evolving.

Moving through a delayed mourning process two years after my mother was consumed by cancer, I spent time with a notebook and many cups of tea, listing the possibilities for being. I jotted down this mix: kind, empathy, learning, standing up for others, artistically expressive, good listener, changing the world for the better, sweet solitude, curious, loves all life, makes people laugh, humility, peaceful, healthy, not weepy, keeping foot out of mouth, etc.

At one point I had loving wife and cat mother, servant-leader, and inspiring writer, but realized those were roles not ways of being. *Being* precedes and supports roles. I then narrowed the list to the elements that most reflected the *Who* in me that wants to become a positive force in the world.

Finally, I wrote a life mission statement in 2005, and except for reframing it as my Becoming Promise, it's never changed.

My Becoming Promise: *I am becoming a person who explores the natural world, nurtures others along my path, and by telling what I learn, expands awareness and empathy.*

It may sound hokey, but this Becoming Promise is the filter through which I make the big decisions and traverse all the little potholes in my life. It's a compass and a conscience. It's a promise to me and to others, because we are all entangled with each other, directly or indirectly. This promise gives me permission to say "no" to many options and requests that don't align with who I want to become. Just as importantly, this promise encourages me to say "yes" to experiences and invitations that, once upon a time, I wouldn't have envisioned for myself.

No worries. You don't have to like my Becoming Promise. It's unique to me and my invisible thread. Am I perfect at keeping my promise? No.

There is no perfect promise, because becoming is always a work in progress.

For you, the question remains: *Who do you want to become?* I'll offer some ideas later in this book to help you answer it. If you've never thought about the question, creating a new life in the midst of loss is a great time to start exploring it.

Can we believe in metamorphosis?

As a wildlife biologist, my husband once collected a chrysalis hanging from a twig and relocated it to a warm, safe spot in our garden as a gift for me. I was truly excited as I'd never had the chance to see with my own eyes how a caterpillar that had turned into a chrysalis then becomes a butterfly. Yes, it doesn't take much to dazzle me.

The chrysalis was a bit drab, colored sooty green and brown, and it dangled on the twig like a crumpled leaf from last autumn that forgot to drop. "That's going to become a lovely Tiger swallowtail?" I asked. It was a little hard to imagine such transformation. Tiger swallowtails are big fluttering beauties with a four-inch wingspan, yellow with black stripes, and bright bluish dots on each hip. Okay, butterflies don't have hips, but that's how I think of them. We looked up the chrysalis in our butterfly book to confirm. Yes!

It was spring, and if all went well, in days or a couple of weeks, we'd be the proud adopted parents of a being that knows how to grow its own wings and sip sweetness from flowers. Every morning before work, I'd slip out to check on "my" butterfly. At first, nothing. I wondered if it was alive or really just an old dead leaf. Still, I had faith.

Beauty can break out of ugliness.

I don't remember how long it took, maybe two or three weeks, and the chrysalis started to take on a translucent quality. I could see there was something magical happening inside. One morning the mass was moving like cats wrestling in a pillowcase. I stood there for more than two hours, barely moving, just the sound of my breath in and out through a stuffy nose, waiting to see her emerge before I had to get to work. I kept thinking, *I can't call in sick. Wonder what would happen if I called in curious and happy?*

No overtime that evening. I dashed home and out into our wooded yard, still in suit and pumps, pantyhose snagging the edge of a garden bench, before my husband could catch up and say, "Too late. I missed it too." There was only an empty twig.

That summer lots of Tiger swallowtails visited us, and I always wondered which one was "mine." In a way, they all were because I loved them all. Yes, I actually felt love and gratitude toward them. They were gifts offered to anyone paying attention, floating like slips of colored wrapping paper in the air. I'd imagine them enduring a metamorphosis that couldn't be easy or feel good. Each had once been a leggy, green, earthbound caterpillar, then its life shrank as it became a strange dead leafy thing. Finally, there it was, a butterfly careening in currents of air, fragile and tough at the same time.

Is it too much to say that being in a state of grief or mourning is like being in a chrysalis that's homely yet holds the unbelievable possibility of wings?

As I live with the reality that my husband is dying as I write, I'm struck by how limited and unfamiliar our life together has become. More than a failing heart, he's dealing with jolts of pain, the torment of persistent tinnitus, weak and wheezy, and now a flaming rash blooming all over his body that itches, stings, and sometimes feels like being mined by ants. I call him my red leopard and say I have three cats in the house now, which makes him smile.

No hikes holding hands, looking and listening for birds. No kicking along our beaches, hauling driftwood together back to the truck. No trimming up the trails he's built through the redwoods on our four acres. No biologist in the kitchen making chicken cacciatore, dancing with his wine. No planning our next trip to the rainforest or desert. No dozing off on his chest with his arm wrapped around me because it hurts to hold me that way. All the surrenders are amplified by the need during this time of expanding COVID-19 to cocoon.

As I ask myself, *Who am I becoming now that the one I love is leaving soon?*, sometimes the only word that comes to me is small.

Small feels deeply sad at times. I don't recognize my life. Small also feels surprisingly hopeful.

When my life-support system kicks in, I feel like the little boy in Ecuador, knowing I can grow "alto." While I'm physically petite, there is a version of tall in my future, there has to be, as I intentionally wind my way through this heart-breaking time, trying to be helpful to others. This chrysalis of impending loss will give way to a more expansive life. The work now is quietly designing what my new wings will look like in this next stage of becoming.

Review:

Stepping Stones to Help You in Your Loss Journey

You are always becoming someone new on multiple levels— physically, mentally, emotionally, and spiritually. While there is the invisible thread at the core of your life that doesn't change, there is always the possibility for renewal and growth.

Who you are includes how you exist in relation to others. You play many roles relative to the people in your life, and those roles change in the face of death. It helps to explore what roles may have changed as a result of your loss.

Even if you think you can't move forward without the one you love, the fact is, time only moves one way and you are literally moving forward.

You can be intentional in guiding your becoming process by asking: Who do I want to Become? The question asks you to consider the kind of person you want to be and the impact you want your life to have.

A Becoming Promise is an intention you set for the Who you want to become moving forward from your loss.

Grief and mourning are like a chrysalis or cocoon, an intermediary step between who you used to be when the one you love was still alive and who you will become now that you need to go on living without them. Loss may feel "ugly," yet a beautiful life can emerge out of it.

6

Practice

Your Loss Story & Feeling Intention

Practicing

In writing this book for you, I want to support you in at least three ways:

1. Introducing Kindred Spirits: By coming along side you, sharing my experiences and others' stories, I want you to feel less alone in your grieving. In talking with others about why they turn to books when mourning, it's clear that even with loving family and friends nearby, each of us is ultimately responsible for our own healing. Hearing others' stories is like having companions on what is otherwise a lonesome journey at times.

2. Conveying Learned Wisdom: By offering insights about loss and mourning, the interplay of body and mind, relationships, expectations, memory, meaning-making, and the constellation of issues that affect how you process a death, I hope you'll spend less time suffering in the darkest corners of grief while inviting joy back into your life sooner.

3. Presenting Simple Practices: By sharing practices in the form of rituals, habits, and mindsets that give you practical and proven actions for nurturing your well-being, I encourage you to develop your unique answer to the question: How do I live with loss without losing myself? The intent is that you'll move forward with your loss to become a vibrant, new version of you.

While the heart of this book focuses on the first two support goals, at the end of each of the four sections, you'll find a **Practice Chapter** like this one. Each Practice Chapter offers step-by-step suggestions or specific strategies for supporting yourself through the ups and downs of integrating loss into your life, creating breaks from grief, and expanding the amount of time you spend experiencing joy every day.

Telling Your Loss Story: Overview

It's time for the first component in building your own, personal life-support system for living with loss: Telling Your Loss Story. It's a two-part process. I'll explain each in more detail, though here's a snapshot:

Part 1: You tell yourself your full Loss Story. Whether you've already told your Loss Story many times or you've avoiding speaking of your loss or you've been shut down by others unable to listen, you need to tell your Loss Story, fully, to you. If you haven't told it all, it needs to be told in order to give yourself your best shot at moving forward. If you're almost tired of telling your Loss Story, you've likely told many versions edited multiple ways depending upon your audience, who is almost never you. While your Loss Story will evolve, you need to listen to the Loss Story that lives in your heart, mind, body, and spirit right now. Later on, we'll explore telling your loss stories to other people or in other ways, but right now, think: This is all about me.

Part II: You set a gentle Feeling Intention for guiding yourself through grief toward a positive what's-next place in your life. I won't ask you to set some big, audacious life goal, but simply trust that joy can be cultivated in your post-death world. I ask you to commit to encouraging joy, or another feeling that's meaningful to you, even in the midst of sorrow, fear, numbness, anger, anxiety, or whatever variety of grief is unfolding. An intention is the proverbial North Star that can shine a little clarity, reminding you of your destination along what is almost always a chaotic, messy trek with loss.

If your loss is very recent or your grief still so raw that telling your story is just too painful right now, then wait until you feel stronger. Read through the rest of the book if it's helpful to you at this point or put it aside. Then, either way, come back to the practices when you are more ready. If at any time in your loss journey you find yourself experiencing thoughts of self-harm, please seek support from a mental health or grief professional, because serious depression can sometimes accompany loss, grief, and mourning. The people who love you, here and gone, want you to live, laugh, and become all you have the potential to become.

Part I: Telling Your Loss Story

I want you to find a place and time where you can be alone and feel safe and comfortable. Be where you can talk to yourself out loud without feeling awkward that others may hear you. I feel nurtured when I'm outdoors in my garden or sitting on a washed-up log on a quiet beach. Others with whom I've shared this process have selected a range of locations: the living room sofa with any other family members off to school or work, an office after hours with the door closed, a friend's basement sewing room, or a car parked in the garage. Ideally, you want to be someplace where you don't have to drive or go anywhere else immediately afterwards. You decide what's best for you—everyone's different.

While I tend to think of private places, one woman that I shared this process with chose a bustling, city-center, coffee-shop patio and wore a Bluetooth headset. She didn't want to be "too alone," and explained that "working in New York, no one pays attention when you talk to yourself. The noise muffles everything, and someone's always crying about something." Apparently, the headset was "a cover" in case a co-worker was wedged in the passing sidewalk crowd.

If being alone is too scary right now, and you have a trusted friend or family member who can sit with you without interrupting or giving feedback during this process, that works, too. It's important, though, that they simply be a supportive presence and not a participant for now.

Make a cup of tea or coffee, grab juice or kombucha, a glass of cool water, or whatever is soothing for you. Skip the wine, beer, or alcohol, along with marijuana and other mood-altering substances, which can magnify emotions and cloud thinking. Morning or afternoon is usually better than evening or night when longing, fears, and despair are more likely to join you. If instrumental music is calming for you (that is, no words or lyrics to intercept your own words), you can include that quietly in your background. Just understand that music can also be emotionally triggering in unexpected ways, so it may or may not be right for you during this process.

Finally, have a notebook and pencil or pen nearby. This is not a journaling exercise, though after you tell your Loss Story you may want to capture key ideas or words. I will later ask you to write down a response to a few questions and capture an intention in writing.

At this point, you are not going to write down your Loss Story. Why? Most people don't feel they are good writers, so writing adds extra stress. Ironically, even those who feel they are good writers can end up sabotaging themselves. You can quickly get caught up in the writing itself, haggling over word choices and self-editing what goes on paper—all of which destroy the power of simply telling your Loss Story. Journaling is a great outlet for working through grief, mourning, and your becoming process, just not for this practice.

Now I want you to tell yourself, out loud, even if it's just a whisper, what happened to the one you loved and to you.

There is no one right way to tell your Loss Story. It may take a typical story format comprising a beginning, middle, and end, with each element told in the sequence in which events unfolded. Frankly, more often loss stories are not tidy, orderly narratives. Instead, they wander a bit, details pop up in the wrong places, and you need to go back or explain a little more. Other times a Loss Story is more like a series of story fragments or short stories tied together, because information is missing for a range of reasons, or some aspects are emotionally more compelling and what happens in between those aspects carries less weight for you.

The only elements I'd like you to keep in mind, in any order or format, are these:

- **Who They Were:** Tell who the person was, saying their name, and explaining their relationship to you. Who were they? Tell about the person you loved and what they were like before they died. If they experienced illness or some life-altering experience prior to their death, be sure to express who they were before their life changed and they died. I want to you spend time on this piece. So often in the early days, weeks, and months after a loss, it's the facts of their death (which you will talk about too) that become lodged in your memory, dominating and crowding out the one you loved. Ultimately, it's not the disturbing reality of their dying, but rather the light of their living that you want to hold on to. Remembering the person in the fullness of their life, their beauty and quirks, keeps them in your life as you move forward, albeit in a different way since they're no longer physically present.

- **What They Were in Your Life:** When they were alive and well, what impact did they have in your life? Tell about your relationship with them. Go beyond simple tags like friend, grandma, son, fur-baby, etc. It's also important to acknowledge both the good and the less-than-perfect influence they had on you. In truth, no one is perfect. Sometimes the people we love hurt us in some way. If you had a complex or difficult relationship, then a very real part of your Loss Story is that, with death, you've lost the possibility of a better relationship with your person. Don't overly focus on the positive or the negative—you're not delivering a eulogy praising them nor a testimony criticizing them. You are speaking holistically about your lost relationship with them. What did that relationship mean in your life and what does it mean now to not have that living relationship?

- **How They Died:** Explain how they died. You may have been with your loved one when it happened or learned of their death afterwards. Whatever your experience of their death was, tell yourself about the death, then how it affected you. Your story may include what they and/or you were doing when it happened, or how others' reactions affected you. There could be facts or details of their death that you don't know or the trauma of loss has hidden them from your memory for now or forever. It's good to acknowledge what you don't know and leave those openings in your story. Over time, those holes may find answers. Whatever you find yourself needing to say, let it flow out of you. Cry, cuss, pace the room like a stressed zoo lion, yell into a pillow, or pause to simply be in the moment—you can be real with you in this process (short of harming yourself or others).

- **Why You Miss Them**: This may at first seem obvious. You miss the one you loved simply because they are gone, right? Here I suggest you play the game of Whys. Ask yourself, why do I miss this person? After you answer that, ask yourself, again, why? Keep going until you run out of Whys. For instance, you might first answer: I miss her because she was my little girl. Why? Because I miss hearing her voice on the phone. Why? Because it reminded me how much I always want to be a mother and that I would always be her mother. Why? Because now I'll never get to plan her wedding or see her become a mother. Why? Because family is such a part of who I am. Why? Because I don't know who I'll love if I don't have her and the family I imagined for her. You get the idea? Why ask why? It will help you identify where and how you are most experiencing the pain of missing your loved one. Asking why helps you zero in on lost roles, unspoken dreams that may be haunting you, changed activities and lost opportunities, and gaps in your days or weeks that you can, eventually, choose how to fill. Asking why also allows you to consider what new experiences you might create as a nurturing response when you find yourself missing your loved one. It's about expressing your love for them in supportive and meaningful ways.

Most people feel almost compelled to tell their Loss Story, so this process, while emotionally and mentally taxing, still unfolds almost effortlessly. When they've finished speaking, they describe feeling like a weight has lifted, at least for a while. Others, like my mother, vehemently avoid talking about their loss even to themselves. I believe unaddressed grief and no real mourning contributed to my mother's lifetime of lost joy. My mother never spoke of her loss, and she seldom had a sense of well-being.

Sometimes a griever feels so tangled up in a mess of details and disbelief they don't know where to begin. When I suggested this process to one woman that I worked with, several months after her partner died, she said she had trouble figuring out how to tell her Loss Story, thinking she had to deliver an organized parable. "The death part," she sighed, "is obviously an ending, but it's also more like a beginning." Good point. A loved one's end is certainly the beginning of a new way of life for you.

Start where it makes sense for you to start, just make sure you start and keep going. You could talk about how they died first, then describe who they were. You might begin with why you miss them and end with what they were in your life. This story is for no one else but you. There's no expectation or judgement, though do address the four areas above.

If you don't know where to start your Loss Story or feel stuck because you know it will be emotionally hard, try telling a brief joy story to yourself first. The woman I just mentioned started developing health issues as she struggled to come to terms with the fact that her partner wasn't coming back and she had two children to raise on her own. She'd not allowed herself to talk about the death, and admitted, "I feel isolated from myself—like I buried me when I buried her."

I asked if she wanted to tell me a story about the most joyful experience in her life. She wasted no time in telling me about the birth of her first daughter. The story was full of fears, drama, and the transformative power of holding her little girl. Then her face opened into a smile as she finished by sharing a funny, new-mother moment, how she'd "freaked out" when a "huge" post-labor drop of sweat landed right in the middle of her newborn's pristine forehead. We both laughed. Not long afterward, she was able to speak her Loss Story to herself, and, she said, "have a hell of a healing cry."

My point? If you are feeling a little overwhelmed about where to start and how to tell your Loss Story, try telling yourself a joy story. The structure of telling a tale of a joyful time often subliminally sets the structure and opens the door for telling your Loss Story. Plus, it's a positive way to start the most challenging story you will ever tell yourself.

After you've finished your storytelling, ask yourself:

- What did it feel like to tell my story?
- How do I feel now?
- How might I feel later on?

Take a moment to acknowledge what you are experiencing physically as well as emotionally. The first time I went through this process, I was exhausted because I cried pretty hard and that always makes me sleepy and headachy. Emotionally, I felt both drained and energized, as if I'd let go of some heavy grief and replaced it with a glimmer of peace.

Grab that notebook, and jot down a quick note about how you felt as soon as your story is complete. If you need to stretch or grab more coffee or a banana, do that and come back to your story space and notebook.

Part II: Your Feeling Intention

Finally, to move forward, it's helpful to set an intention that can guide you in becoming a new you who lives with loss yet knows joy.

Almost everything you do begins with intention, whether you realize it or not. Yes, some actions are reflexive. If a baseball is streaking toward your face, you'll react by ducking or stepping out of the way. You don't stop to ponder or announce your intention to avoid having a ball of cork and leather slam into your face, your brain and body automatically conspire to protect you and don't need your mind's ideas about it. But. Most of what you do starts as an intention.

For example, you're going to make a cup of coffee, pour milk over cereal you put in a bowl, bend forward to greet your dog, and glance at the clock on the microwave to see if you've got time for a run before work. These all start as intentions, though over time you don't feel the intentions—they become the seemingly spontaneous habits or routine of your morning.

While losing someone you love was not any intention of yours, it will take intention to craft a new life without them that includes fulfilling your dreams, goals, and potential.

Who do I want to become?

I'm not asking you to try answering that big question now. There is another question, however, that, once answered, will lay some of the foundation for framing the *Who* you may want to become.

How do I want to feel?

Having told your Loss Story, you're likely experiencing a range of feelings, physically and emotionally, along with a whirl of mental and

92

spiritual disruption. Take a deep, slow breath, and think beyond the current moment. Looking to tomorrow and to the days, weeks, and months ahead, how would you like to feel most of the time during most of your days?

Anytime you are looking to transform some element of your life, setting an intention dramatically increases the likelihood that you'll succeed. When you are mourning, an intention related to feeling happy and whole can offer hope and inspire you to keep slogging forward even on the hardest days. Setting an intention is a goal and a filter. When you're making decisions, you can assess what choices will bring you closer to your intention.

How do I want to feel?

Here are some feeling intentions others have identified: Happy, peaceful, light-hearted, grounded, ambitious, focused, healthy, energized, glowing, joyful, centered, comforted, compassionate, assertive, resilient, gracious, kind, relaxed, vibrant, optimistic, content, well-balanced, inspired, involved in life, self-reliant, enthusiastic, eager, loving, excited, blissful, encouraged, stable, curious, perky, creative, unlimited, caring, trusting, faithful, empowered, purposeful, daring, fearless, easy-going, teachable, going-with-the-flow, self-reflective, grateful, serene, calm, confident, intuitive, perceptive, worthy, adaptable, tolerant, tranquil, accepting, mindful, and the list could go on. So, you have options!

Don't overthink this simple question: How do I want to feel? Just ask it, ideally out loud, and see what answer pops up. You are going to decide in a word or brief phrase how you want to feel and set a Feeling Intention. It shouldn't take more than a couple of minutes.

There are a few guidelines for your Feeling Intention:

- **It's Positive:** Select a word or brief phrase that focuses on the positive. In other words, if the first thought that comes to mind is not stressed-out, reframe the feeling with an affirming term. Instead of not stressed, you might select relaxed, healthy, unshakeable, or mellow to capture the feeling you're aiming for.

- **You Influence It:** Whatever you select as your desired feeling, it needs to be independent of anyone else. While you can't always control how you feel, especially during times of crisis, you are influencing your feelings all the time, whether you realize it or not. With intentional practice, you can gain more power to shift how you feel. If you think you'll never be truly happy again because it was your loved one who made you happy, well, I've felt that way at times, too, but it's just not true (unless there's a serious health issue at play). You can miss someone forever and you can feel inspired or peaceful or grounded every day. Just because loss comes along with you wherever you go, doesn't mean joy can't come along, too—even if it doesn't seem possible now. Ultimately, we make ourselves happy and cultivate our own joy, then loving relationships may amplify those feelings. If you haven't before, this is a good time to take control for how you feel away from others and give it back to you.

- **You Believe in It and Let It Go:** Whatever you select as your Feeling Intention, believe—better yet, know—you will create that feeling as a regular component of your life. Don't narrow your choices or set your intention low because you don't believe you could ever feel that way consistently again. Right now, you don't need to worry about how you'll get to that place or nurture that feeling in your life. Aim for what you really want to feel, believe in it, and let go of expectations beyond that.

Once you have your word or brief phrase, your Feeling Intention, make your own version a fortune cookie, minus the cookie. First, write it on a slip of paper, fold it up, and put it some place meaningful to you, like a treasure and a prediction, which is exactly what it is. This ritual tells your mind and body, overtly and subliminally, that your intention is a valuable asset.

Then write your Feeling Intention on a few (or many) slips of paper, or better, little sticky notes. Put your intention in places where you'll see it, such as the bathroom mirror, orange juice carton, edge of the computer monitor, car dashboard, anywhere that you are bound to see it frequently.

I guarantee that every so often you'll stumble onto one of those slips or sticky notes when you are caught in a rough patch or surfing a grief wave, and it will make you pause, smile, and remember where you're going. You can use the note to try summoning your Feeling Intention into that immediate moment. Say or whisper, "I want to feel _____ (whatever you've chosen for your feeling)." Sometimes you'll be able to shift your mood at least a little, other times not, and along the way you'll get better at feeling better.

Over time, some decide their initial Feeling Intention didn't quite capture what they wanted in their lives. More often, what they wanted evolved through practice. You may start out wanting to feel hopeful, and as you start feeling hopeful more often, you then decide you want to aim for feeling empowered. The point is to pick a feeling that's meaningful to you now and aim your intentions to get to that feeling. I want you to know this simple step will change you in ways you can't imagine right now.

Section 2

Reinhabiting your animal body

7

Loving

Love doesn't end with loss

To love, is to be a moon, a silvery stone suspended in orbit around the beloved. If that circle is broken, there may only be the void, the hissing static of space. So you hold on to that worn groove, round and round, such a happy rut.

— from my notebooks, March 2015

Love is a habit. Say it with me, okay? Love is a habit. And how we love people takes shape in countless tiny rituals. I bet you've never looked at love that way, as a habit and set of rituals.

Love. It's an emotion, yes, but also action, mostly automatic, a habit. When someone asks you why you love them, you can probably come up with a list of their traits that make them lovable. But let's be honest. Do you really know why you love anyone? The intellect doesn't have all the answers.

You just love. I've never been pregnant, but it's proof that that love doesn't need to know why. Countless times I've watched colleagues, staff, and friends moving through their pregnancy. At some point, they almost all developed a habit of rubbing their round belly without thinking about it, sensing the shift and kick of an inner being they've never met yet are visibly loving.

The people we love, and at least for me the animals, too, create the contours and margins of our lives, contributing to the depth and points of pleasure in our days. Yes, our loved ones can also contribute to some of our worry and frustration, even our self-doubt through the expectations they place on us. Regardless, their presence in our lives is a fundamental habit, part of the daily routine that is ultimately you and me.

You get up each morning and surely have a series of habits and rituals, a routine, that move you into the day. Let's say you wake up, you take your little trip to the latrine, splash water on your face, and head to the kitchen to feed the cats and make a cup of tea. Then you start a pot of coffee for your sweetheart or decide whether it's PBJ or cheese and crackers for your son's lunchbox today or make a note to call Mom for your daily check in and to ask if it's okay to swap canned tomatoes for fresh in grandma's marinara. Okay, your morning routine has different elements, but you get the idea, right?

When the one you love is gone—your partner, your parent, your child, your sibling, your friend, your furred or feathered companion—when their physical presence is vanished, it's as if some invisible blade just severed a leg or two from the chair you're sitting on. You come crashing to the ground, unbalanced, hurt, and that structure—the chair that here is the metaphor for your life—is utterly broken.

Now you get up each morning, no choice on the little trip to the latrine—you have to do that. But do you reach for the faucet or bother to look at your own face in the bathroom mirror? I know, scary. Hopefully you think to feed the cats. Robotically you put on water for a cup of tea, and while the water spits and swirls in the kettle, you're too numb to even think, now what? Still, you feel it viscerally, don't you, your body screams it: Now what?

Habits and rituals are like stepping stones that lead you through each day. When the one you love, the habit of them in your life and the rituals of loving them are gone—forever—it's easy to feel literally lost.

Did you know that love notes can lead to broken mornings?

A little love note, newly written, was folded on a plate. That's how Livia topped off her morning routine before jumping in the car, tall tumbler of coffee in hand, and heading off to work. She left the plate with the note on the kitchen counter for her husband to find when he woke up. On weekends, the note got tucked alongside toast and whatever else she served him for breakfast.

Livia and her husband were one of those couples who found each other in college, drifted apart, married other people, divorced, and became single parents. In their late 40s, kids off to college, they ran into each other sizing up the organic mushrooms at a natural foods store. From the moment I first met Livia, she had to tell me how much she loved her husband, how they'd had a "real" love affair. "We were both holding up one of those little portobellos," she shared, her hand in the air as if holding an invisible mushroom. "We were literally feet apart after decades apart. We both felt it, you know, that electricity."

After a short courtship, they didn't want to waste any more time, so they married in a friend's backyard, merged households, and travelled whenever they weren't working. "We were all about snorkels and palm trees," Livia told me, closing her eyes as if submerging herself in one of her memories of Hawaii or Fiji. A few years into their happy union, her husband developed a complex and never fully diagnosed health condition that left him with pain, balance issues that could topple him to the ground, and a kind of brain fog. He had to accept disability and leave a career he was still excitedly building. The love of Livia's life could manage on his own during the day while she was at work, but he quickly grew depressed, anxious, and bitter, which seemed to accelerate his decline.

Livia started crafting her little love notes shortly after he left his job. "I wanted to lift his spirits," she explained, "and remind him I adored him no matter what." She started writing a note every morning, coming up with some phrase or sketch or mini-memory to convey *I Love You* in a new way. Once it was a crayon drawing of them snorkeling with bright orange fish and a heart. One October, she folded in a colorful fall leaf each morning. She also had a ritual of calling her husband at lunchtime to check in. The days and then years went by like that, until one evening he couldn't breathe. In a matter of frantic moments, he was gone.

Livia was about six months into widowhood when I first sat down with her to discuss the memorial she wanted to create for her husband. She told her Loss Story stoically. When I asked her about the notes, if she missed doing them, her face seemed to collapse, and tears came. Yes, I was immediately sorry I asked that question, but then, it turned out to be a question she needed to answer. I grabbed a box of tissues from her powder room and just sat with her.

After awhile, she said something I'll never forget. "Maybe all those love notes were really for me." She explained that it wasn't just her husband who'd become disabled, "Our whole lives were disabled." Their kids in other states, Livia struggled to balance work, taking care of her husband, grocery shopping and cooking, household chores, mowing the

102

lawn, fixing whatever wasn't working, and trying to stretch one income to hang on to their mortgage and pay medical bills. "He had to die for me to have the money from his 401k, IRA, and life insurance to be able to pay everything off and have a little left to do something to keep him alive, a memorial."

The morning after her husband died, Livia described how not having a reason to write one of her notes felt like falling down a well with no bottom. An enormous, endless hole. She noticed a receipt lying by her purse, grabbed it, flipped it over, and wrote one word in black marker, "*uck!" It was her last note, aimed at a seemingly random universe.

She'd taken a little time off after her husband's death, sleeping in and tackling the logistics and financial maneuvering that come with the loss of a spouse. All the busyness helped contain her grief. At home in those early days, there was an altered flow to her experience of time, and built-up exhaustion mercifully allowed her to sleep.

Unfortunately, going back to work was a huge grief trigger. It meant a return to a routine that was broken. After making her morning tumbler of coffee, she found herself pausing in that tiny time when she used to design a love note. She'd feel her heart start fluttering arrhythmically in her chest like a flailing, injured bird, followed by pangs of nausea. She started skipping breakfast and worked through lunch to avoid the absence of her husband's voice on the phone. Nights were sobbing into a bowl of cereal then sitting wide awake in bed half the night. She gave a half-hearted laugh when she told me, "It's a great weight-loss program, but I wouldn't recommend it."

We are, in part, our rituals, habits, and routines.

Maybe you don't write love notes every morning, but what are the tiny rituals and ingrained habits that comprised your daily routine when the one you loved was still a physical presence in your life? Where are the little as well as the big gaps in your day now?

Habits and rituals together are the stepping stones that move us through each day, week, month, and year. We are what we regularly do, and what we regularly do involves other people (and animal companions, too). We tend to think of a routine as boring. But. Routine helps us feel grounded and secure.

When a death dismantles the fundamental pattern to your daily life, your ability to move forward through time and space is also dismantled. It's like suddenly finding yourself at a raging river just in time to watch the bridge torn apart and swept away.

Let's take a moment to talk about rituals, habits, and routines.

A routine is a series or sequence of habits and rituals that you follow consistently. Maybe you brush your teeth, wash your face, then comb your hair every morning before sitting on the edge of your son's bed, kissing his temple, and whispering, "Time to wake up."

A ritual? Often when I use the word ritual, people think purely in religious terms, like communion or bedtime prayers. Yes, those are rituals, but most rituals are about attention not religion. A ritual is an action done repeatedly with a purpose bigger than the action itself.

Morning love notes certainly fit the definition. There's the act of jotting down a message, but the act is done with a larger purpose, conveying to someone else that they are loved. At the same time, when you express love to someone else, you feel good, and that's the beauty of a good ritual.

A ritual is a kind of knot that ties that invisible thread that is your life to someone else's.

Other rituals? A hug before bed. Sharing stories about how the day went and listening, really listening, to each other. Holding hands on the evening walk. Warming up the car before her snowy drive. Laying out his shirt and just the right tie the night before. Ensuring a certain stuffed bunny or dinosaur cup makes it into the van. Catching fireflies and sharing the magic of pulsing light in your child's cupped hands. Watching the sun set into the earth with your sweetheart, following its yellow glow as it turns reddish then dissolves as a dot on the horizon, together.

Habits are similar, but less intentional. A habit is an action done repeatedly for the sake of the action itself. Habits tend to have a more negative connotation, because many of our habits are behaviors that aren't good for us. Think: nail biting, hitting the snooze alarm and running late, making a taco run before bed, and checking your smartphone and social media constantly.

Most habits are actually constructive. We'll also be more successful at breaking bad habits if we focus on creating good ones. In fact, energizing habits often begin as rituals, started with purpose, then repeated until they become automatic.

For a brief time after I left home at 19, I smoked, not socially like most beginning smokers, but when I was alone, likely to stave off the aloneness. I knew it was dumb. As soon as I was home from classes and work, solo in my studio apartment, the slender, menthol cigarettes were so seductive. *Quick, where are the matches?*

On another level, I wanted to be more active, so I started walking almost every morning. Walking got me out in fresh air, my blood pumping and my muscles flexing. I met up with the local dogs and befriended a certain grey and white cat who waited for me, knowing I'd pause to pet her. I saw how the same walk is never the same walk. Flowers sprouted, bloomed, and withered out of a specific sidewalk crack. Balmy mornings became brisk. A park full of leafy sycamores turned into a stand of naked white trunks, their branches against the slatey clouds looking like roots in the sky.

I didn't realize it then, but the move from being teenage kid living with her family to that of a young woman out on her own was a type of loss, letting go of one identity and routine in the process of becoming the next version of myself. The challenge was how to replace the nightly chores and connections tied to living with my parents to being an adult who can choose how to fill a few hours before bed.

Fortunately, it didn't take long to realize I didn't want to erode the benefits of my morning walk with a nightly smoke. Walking nurtured my well-being, so why keep firing up that evening cigarette that only turned my two-room studio into a hazy cave? I started giving my attention to an old, oak, upright piano I'd hauled from home, bought because I wanted to become a composer. The nights moved from feeling lost and off-center to being creative if a little off-key (I couldn't afford piano tuning). My smoking habit lasted less than six months, the piano-composing ritual that replaced it eventually gave way to poetry writing, and my walking routine, well, it's lasted a lifetime.

It helps to be mindful of what's missing.

When loss comes along, we need to pay attention to the way our habit of loving someone and the rituals around that love have been ruptured. Otherwise, it will be hard to move forward through each day, and we can inadvertently develop new habits and rituals that further erode or work against our possibility for well-being.

Recently I talked with Brittany, the adult daughter of a donor I used to work with. I'd heard my donor's husband had been very sick but didn't know he died. Brittany called to see if I knew whether her mother had moved forward with a memorial for her father. Having changed positions to work with a different charity, I had no idea. She then shared her Loss Story about her father, then described a second Loss Story. She felt like she lost her mother when her father died.

Brittany's parents were successful, small-business owners. When her father became terminally ill and unable to lead their business, her mother jumped in with both feet keeping the business running while being her father's caregiver. When he died, she admitted it was a relief for her and her mother, because he was living with pain, severe disability, and no real quality of life. They were all together in the final moments, holding hands, telling him they'd miss him but they'd okay. Months of suffering gave way to peace.

In the immediate days after he was gone, she and her mother spent time together, consoling each other. They enjoyed little daily adventures in the open spaces in her mother's schedule that no longer needed to be spent in caregiving. There were long lunches out, yoga at the art museum, a random movie, and a slow hike around a lake they hadn't visited since she was a child. "We got totally muddy. It was great."

Eventually, Brittany, who lived in another state, had to get back home and to her job. Within a few weeks, her mother became a workaholic. Brittany could hear the hustle and fatigue on the phone, yet whenever she tried to talk to her mother about the need to grieve and mourn, her mother shut her down. "Too busy" with the business, she said, to "talk about that." Months later, when Brittany flew home for the holidays, she had to let herself in the front door with a key hidden in a planter. Her mother didn't arrive until nearly midnight. When she came through the door, Brittany was horrified. "She was emaciated," Brittany told me, "like a person from a country at war, only in a gorgeous suit that hung loose and baggy."

At breakfast the next morning, her mother admitted she was exhausted and needed time to herself, but it was impossible because the business needed her. Brittany pointed out that her mother was able to run the business without the long hours when she was caring for her father. What happened to all those hours caring for the man they both loved and lost, that could be spent in so many ways in his absence?

I haven't heard from Brittany since that call, but before we hung up, I shared how she might help her mother begin to find time in her day by starting with a practice I call "Tiny-Come-Back-to-Your-Senses Rituals." Brittany loved the idea. As we brainstormed, she came up with a Tiny-Come-Back-to-Your-Senses Ritual that she and her mother could share, and they'd begin during a visit a couple of weeks later. It would be a ritual they could continue even when apart, so they could help each other be accountable to caring for themselves. "If this works, maybe I can slowly get her out of the office, and back to the lake. She was so happy there."

When we lose people we love, especially if we've been in caregiving mode in the preceding weeks, months, or years, there can be a huge emptiness to our days. We miss our people. We miss all the little moments in the day when we were with them or thought about them or thought about being with them again. We even miss the awful moments with them, because those, too, meant they were still with us and gave a place to focus our love.

What will fill the gaps and gaping holes in your day now that your person, or beloved animal, is gone? What if you could repurpose those vacant moments to help you take a break from grief and hold space for joy to enter into your days?

Tiny-Come-Back-to-Your-Senses Rituals are a foundational step in my life-support system for living with loss, and I'll share how to create them later in this section. The good news is that a tiny sensory ritual initially takes only three minutes. Whether you're an emaciated, workaholic trying to keep one step ahead of your grief, or you feel utterly immobile, barely able to get out of bed, as if every bit of energy has drained from your body, this healing practice is doable.

You can't help loving.

Love is a habit. How did I realize that? A dying dove was my teacher. This may sound a bit strange, but I've held a number of birds as they died. Fortunately, I've held many more who were only dazed, eventually fluttering up and away, apparently okay.

My husband is a retired wildlife biologist, so no matter where we've lived, it involved a house with many windows adjacent to forests. When you live like that, you're going to find fallen birds. Deceived by the reflection of trees, they slam into glass. Whenever I hear that dreadful thud, I dash around looking for a flailing, unconscious, or dying bird. At the risk of sharing too much information, let me also admit that the dead ones, wrapped in plastic, sometimes end up in my freezer. In death, they've become models for my husband's woodcarvings of birds or they go to the university to be used as study skins by wildlife students. They have a second life.

Thinking of some of the fallen ones I've held, warms my palms, remembering the bodies and birdy faces: Red crossbill, Dark-eyed junco, American robin, Eastern bluebird, Anna's and Ruby-throated hummingbirds, Goldfinch, Pine siskin, Fox sparrow, Plain titmouse, and the big, meaty frame of a Band-tailed pigeon, the wild, migrating relative of city pigeons. I never like finding a downed bird, but I can't help the delight in seeing the iridescent feathers up close and admiring the various beaks, tough and fragile. I've looked into the differing, round eyes like shiny portals to another place. Who can't marvel at how spectacularly creative the natural world is to make so many colorful, flighty beings? Who doesn't want to touch what is usually untouchable?

One afternoon, the thud was a Mourning dove. She mistook the window of my home office for a shortcut into the woods, hitting the glass so hard it startled one of my cats to leap out of sleep onto the floor.

When I lifted the dove's body out of the flower bed, cradling her limp neck, I could feel the hidden flutter of her heart beating fast. Still alive. I was relieved.

I sat with her on the porch, her slender form stretching across both palms. Gently stroking her sandy-pink shoulders, I looked into her open left eye, a liquid black bead held within a circle of bright, periwinkle-blue. For more than 20 minutes, we stayed together. I could sense her dying. The little engine of her life slowed then stopped. A few minutes more, and her eye lost the shine of living. It was time to nestle her in leaves, wish her Godspeed, and tell my husband all about her.

Instead, surprise, I found myself crying a little. I thought, *Why do I do this? Why do I run for these fallen ones? Why expose myself to grieving a bird?*

You know what brief answer flitted through my bird-focused brain? *Love habit.* It's a habit grown out of loving my bird-curious husband.

When I'm holding a bird, whether it lifts on its wings or the light goes out of its eyes, I experience it all as if my husband is with me. We are experiencing the wonder, an excitement toward all life, from birds to salmon and mountain lions to banana slugs.

This is one love habit I know won't break when my husband dies and I'm missing him. Inevitably, random birds will take their wrong turns and end up in my palms. I'll do what I can to nurture them back into the sky. *We* will marvel at the artistry in those wings.

Review:
Stepping Stones to Help You in Your Loss Journey

Love is a habit, and how you love others takes shape in a range of daily rituals and routines. A significant part of your life is lived in relationship to others, which is why we can feel lost in many ways.

A ritual is an action done repeatedly with a purpose bigger than the action itself. A habit is an action done repeatedly for the sake of the action itself. A routine is a series or sequence of habits and rituals that you follow consistently.

When the one you love is gone, your days and weeks can feel broken. The rituals and routines that involved your loved one no longer work, so your life essentially stops working.

The gaps in your daily routines that involved others become major grief triggers. It helps to identify the gaps, then create new rituals and habits to bridge those gaps.

Some habits and rituals tied to the one you love won't break with their death, and if you identify those, they can nurture you through the times when you are missing your beloved person or animal.

8

Relating

You are, in part, your relationships

*What is hell? You read it is the last bee in the blossom, then unrelenting hunger.
Maybe. Real suffering is moving through your days, never hearing your name spoken, the ones who knew you quiet as dirt.*

— from my notebooks, May 2019

In the night, a Barred owl began calling in the redwoods outside the
bedroom, the window cracked to let in cool, misty air and apparently
the voice of this seldom seen bird talking to himself. Birders hear the
Barred owl's call as, "Who cooks for you?"

Sleepless in bed, following the strange tempo of my husband's la-
bored breathing, I heard the owl asking, "Who looks for pearls?" The

"pearls" part was a gravelly, downward trill, a husky cat purr trailing off into silence. A few moments later he offered his owlish question again, the rattle-purr once more falling away. *Who looks for Purrrrrrrrlz?*

My husband is an owl biologist, so owls are a spirit animal for us. As the owl called and paused, called and paused, my husband, half asleep, whispered, "Do you hear it?" Tiger cat heard it, too, jumping up in bed, tail whipping the quilt, curious. Then, surprise, in the distance and faint, another Barred owl responded, the voice rhythmically different, likely his companion. Barred owls mate for life unless something happens to one of them. As the owls conversed through the wide space of night and density of trees, it dawned on me how my husband moves farther away from me with each passing day.

A foot and a half tall, Barred owls compete for the same habitat as the endangered Spotted owl, so some environmentalists despise them. But. The world is defined by time and change. I say an owl is no different from you or me, flying through its own versions of loss and resilience. There's so much dying on this planet, so any owl is a thrilling gift.

Eyes closed, I imagined the owls' mottled, brown feathers in the shadowy branches. Tucked against the upper trunks of a redwood or spruce, they look like tree bark until they spread their wings, lift, and vanish into stars. Such magic and possibility.

Rituals can go rogue.

Listening to my husband breathe as I wait for sleep is a new ritual for me the last few years. I focus on it, as if it's an audible map that will tell me where we're going next in what time we have left together. As I think about this ritual, I realize it's a paradox, being both comforting and disturbing. His breath says, *I'm here.* And also, *I'm slowly falling apart.* Strange, but I know I'll miss even these moments of anxious knowing, aware that death will come, but hasn't yet.

Before. I try to hold on to this odd place of *before*, as in, cherish these moments *before* he's gone. Honor even the times that are hard and sad, maybe even awful. But you know what? From the second we're born, we're all in *before*. Why does it take illness and loss to remind us of that?

In considering the mixed emotions this particular ritual triggers, I want to tell you: beware of rituals that may not be entirely positive. Some rituals contain elements of distress, anger, shame, and conflict.

A professor I once worked with thought he'd moved forward pretty well from the loss of his son, who was coming home from a Bible-study group when he was rammed head-on by a drunk driver. After a couple weeks' leave, Professor was back teaching, explaining and unpacking science concepts, talking about natural history and evolution, and coaching his students through fieldwork.

Then a student started challenging him in the classroom, making a case for creationism. This professor was the type who had always encouraged critical thinking and challenging the theories he taught. He'd engaged his classes in animated debates of evolution versus creationism many times, encouraging students to draw and defend their own conclusions. This time, though, the professor told me, "I'm stuck. I can't speak. I stand there like an idiot, the students waiting for me to say something. My heart and head pound. All I want to do is bolt for the door."

As I got to know this professor, he shared his Loss Story, and I understood how deeply he and his son loved each other. He was candid in saying how surprised he was when his son, as a teenager, became a Born-Again Christian. He said it didn't matter to him what his son believed so long as "he asked good questions first to know it made sense." Being a professor, he gave me a free lesson on the scientific method of observation, inquiry, and hypothesis-testing. Then he talked about a ritual he and his son developed. When his son came home from his weekly Bible study groups on Thursday evenings, the two of them would grab a glass of milk and debate what his son had discussed in the group.

The weekly debates became a seven-year-long ritual, continuing most weeks even after his son left home—they were that close. Mostly a shared, enjoyable intellectual exercise, sometimes both tempers flared. Occasionally the dialogue deteriorated into criticism, ending with a door slam or worse, an "unkind epithet," in other words, name-calling.

A few days before the car accident, Professor and son had one of their heated verbal jousts. A few days afterward, Thursday came again but without his son. All he could think about were the last ugly words of that final conversation.

In the early days of grief, this loving but highly charged ritual was, as he put it, "haunting the hell" out of him. Within a few weeks, his wife deftly converted the Thursday debate night into a date night. While still mourning his son, he found the familiarity of teaching and research mostly good therapy. Still, his anxiety raged. I assumed he was getting lost in the interactions with his faith-oriented student, because it reminded him of his own son.

I was only partially right. Sitting across from Professor over a lunch meeting, I asked him how the semester was going. After talking about campus budget woes and politics, he said, "I'm mostly back." He was doing better, if a bit clumsy, in working with the questioning student.

"It dawned on me," he said, "that my son was trying to save me." He paused, looking around to make sure I was the only one leaning in. "It wasn't just an intellectual debate for him like it was for me. I think he was trying hard to save his old man's soul."

Connections to others depend so heavily on words, how we understand them and misunderstand them—both the words and the person.

When loss comes along, there aren't any more opportunities to ask the one you love, "Hey, what did you mean?"

Rituals that come with hurt are the most likely to leave you emotionally marooned. They can also be tricky to pinpoint as a roadblock to moving forward. As you look at where you are in your loss journey, I encourage you to look for all the rituals that may be broken in your daily and weekly routines—the simple nurturing ones as well as the ones that may have involved conflict or discord with your loved one.

Out of one loss, come many griefs.

In the summer of 1996, I spent two-and-a-half days interviewing to be the first paid CEO of a then 81-year-old community foundation in Williamsport, Pennsylvania, best known as the birthplace of Little League Baseball. Looking back, I'm stunned that a young, 30-something woman, living in California would be a finalist for such a major job in a conservative community. Maybe the search committee was, too, because I was thoroughly grilled. Interview sessions ran breakfast through dinner, involving a range of community leaders.

A former board member and his wife were my caretakers during the process. As we drove to the first meal, they asked me to be flexible with the flow of interviewing because the community had just lost 21 people. Funerals and memorials were planned over many days. A group of 16 high school French students and 5 adult chaperones from nearby Montoursville were on TWA Flight 800 when it exploded and plunged into the Atlantic off the coast of Long Island, NY, on July 17th of that year.

Sure enough, as I answered questions and made presentations, there were a few people in each session who would get up, nod at me, and quietly slip out of a door. Their grief was visible in their faces. I was honored that they would even attend an interview proceeding in the midst of what was clearly an emotional marathon as many in the community attended memorial after memorial.

What I didn't know as I sat in all those interviews, my mind focused on good answers and my heart tuned into the background of communal pain, is that the most poignant and meaningful period of my career would be working with many of the families who'd lost a child or a wife or a sibling on Fight 800.

The crash was a major story at the time, and media rushed in with cameras and microphones, initially making it hard for families and the region to express their sorrow in peace. Adding to the trauma was the possibility the flight was brought down as a terrorist act or a friendly-fire accident of a military exercise. Many donations flowed in from around the country and the world in support of the families affected and to honor their lost loved ones.

By the time I arrived as the community foundation's first full-time leader, there were two pools of donated monies held on behalf of the families. There were also the beginnings of what would be significant stresses between families as well as within families about the most appropriate ways to apply the funds for immediate needs, like funeral costs, and as a legacy to the lost.

In the early months of my time in Williamsport, then stretching into years, I listened to mothers, fathers, sisters and brothers, an aunt or two, and one husband tell their loss stories. There was so much more behind the newspaper vignettes of each student and adult, encapsulating a life in a tidy paragraph or two with a photo. A Loss Story is about a relationship, so it's always about at least two people: the one gone and the one who keeps on going. Our lives knot together, and death doesn't really unravel that knot. Sometimes, though, the knots between survivors turn into snares.

What moved me, still moves me now, was what was happening inside some of the families as they confronted their loss. While disagreements between families about how to use the charitable funds made the local paper, I knew issues of money would resolve with talk and time, and the Foundation's board and I could be neutral facilitators as needed.

The strange gift that came with my new position was an intimacy with others' grief. My professional role was to help families explore meaningful options for memorializing the ones they loved. I'm I human being, though, before I'm anything else. Against the glare of reporters looking for printable stories every July 17th and a sense that the world wanted accountability for those donated dollars, I wanted to be at least one positive force in those families' lives that was there, privately and without expectation, to be supportive.

Oddly, watching my parents' marriage disintegrate over the years following the fire turned out to be good credentials for my job. I witnessed personal struggles and internal turmoil as husbands, wives, and children responded to their loss in often dramatically different ways.

I can still hear one mother's voice, "How can my husband just get up and go to work when our daughter is dead and is never coming home? He seems so cold and in his own world." Talking to her husband sometime later, he shared, "I'm worried about my wife. The crying doesn't stop. It's as if she's frozen in time. I miss my daughter more than I can express, but we need to pay the mortgage. We have to go on anyway."

Some of us hide our grief and some of us hide in our grief. That reality can spark serious friction in a family, a handful of friends, or a community.

It's one thing for me to say to you, we all grieve differently and that's okay, that's as it should be. You can see that, right? But. When people grieve in disparate and seemingly opposing ways within a family, well,

119

let's just say, at least a few families were as broken apart as that plane in the aftermath of Flight 800.

Why do I share this? When we lose someone we love, more often than not, someone else also loved them. As desperately alone as we may feel in our grief, there are usually others grieving their own version of the same loss. Most of the time, we don't have to grapple with loss before a global audience, but even the introverts among us (that includes me) have a circle of diverse others around them.

While it's good to give yourself permission to grieve exactly in the way you need to, unless it involves harming yourself or other people, are you granting that permission to others?

I know—I hear you. If you're suffering with grief, why do you have to worry about others' grief? You'd don't need to fix anyone else's pain, but it will help you if you acknowledge their mourning is on a separate path than yours. The people you love may not only be unable to support you, understandably, you're probably unable to support them, too. That's okay, but pause before you push each other away. For me, often it wasn't the people closest to me who could help me survive loss, but more distant others.

It was my mother-in-law Rose who was most there for me emotionally in the immediacy of my mother's dying. My much younger brother and sister were a continent away and had their own, distinct relationships with my mother. We shared the same major loss, yet mourned as if we each lost a different mother. My husband wanted to be supportive, though he didn't understand my desolation and longing given the complicated relationship my mother and I shared. The longer my grief stretched, ultimately two years, the less he understood. Through it all, though, I knew I would eventually reach the other side of unrelenting grief and that I'd want him waiting for me there.

It's not about being magnanimous with others or simply cutting them slack when they can't be there for you in the dark hours after a death, though those can be helpful coping strategies. I'm saying, be a little selfish in a good way.

The goal is well-being and the ability to cultivate joy in your days again. When you dwell on others' emotional-support shortcomings and, feeling abandoned, nudge them away, you are creating more loss and inviting the kaleidoscope of desperate feelings to dig you a deeper grief hole. If anyone is actually abusive, yes, cut that cord and fast, though usually that's not the case.

You'll fare better in your mourning by keeping the close, if imperfect, relationships that shaped your life before death visited you. Sometimes death exposes problems that were always there and can't be reconciled. Other times, death reminds you that despite your differences, you and your people need each other. Down the road, when you can see and feel more clearly, you can always root out those relationships that truly don't work anymore.

Are you experiencing emotional inertia?

Do you have a good idea of where you are in your loss journey? Are you in the early, raw-grief period and just beginning to wonder what's next? Or are you caught in loss limbo, acknowledging that the one you love is gone forever, but floating through your days on automatic pilot, feeling a bit hollow and directionless?

Wherever you are on your loss journey, I want you to ask yourself: What's holding me back right now?

I've shared so many conversations about death and dying with others over the years, women especially, and when I ask that question, often they're stumped. They talk about a lack of stamina and motivation, a feeling that nothing matters anymore, and a sense of overwhelming hopelessness, even doom.

Trying to live after loss is like waking up at the base of a steep mountain. Everything seems immense, draining, and undoable, even if it's a task as simple as scrambling an egg. Sound familiar? I certainly skipped a few breakfasts after my mother died because I just couldn't muster the energy to even tap an eggshell with the edge of a knife.

When rituals, habits, and routines fracture, they allow an opening to something corrosive. Emotional inertia.

Remember your high school science or college physics lessons? I'm a little geeky about natural science, but bear with me. There's a concept called The Law of Inertia. It goes like this—things in motion tend to stay in motion and things at rest tend to stay at rest, at least until acted upon by some force. It's how you go from watching one episode of Seinfeld, to watching six, and then dozing off on the couch. It's also how, once you start looking for something in a cluttered cupboard in the garage, you end up reorganizing the entire garage and cleaning all the doorknobs.

How can we be the same people, still as a stone one day and the definition of momentum the next?

When we're living with loss, it's easy to develop a nasty case of emotional inertia, where we're stuck either in perpetual motion or languishing in immobility. Either way, we're unable to move our lives toward balance and well-being. Emotional inertia is real, and it's more than emotional, because it can impact our bodies and our health. I developed autoimmune conditions, so yes, best to limit extremes of too much or too little action.

Emotional inertia shows up in multiple forms. The active, can't-stop-or-I'll-crash version happens when we try to bury ourselves and our grief in busyness. We fill every moment with overtime and extra shifts, focusing all our attention on our kids or an aging parent to the exclusion of ourselves, serving on committees and volunteering for every odd project, moving like a hurricane until and unless a force breaks that momentum, like sheer exhaustion.

More often, though, women living with loss tell me they feel like bears drawn to hibernation. If there is a spirit animal for me, it's surely the bear, even more than the owl, though the bearish traits I'd most want to embody are strength, wisdom, and protectiveness of others, not sleeping for months in a snow cave.

Perhaps you've experienced the lethargic version of emotional inertia. It's foggy, confused thinking and the inability to make a decision. It's saying "no" to every opportunity to do something you always enjoyed or be with friends or family who used to make you laugh. It's being late for work, deadlines, and picking up the kids. It's a to-do list that doesn't get done from dentist appointments to the oil change, that nagging light in the dashboard we learn to ignore. It's the dog's water bowl running dry. It's piles—of laundry, dishes, bills, newspapers, and fallen leaves cluttering the front door. There's nothing wrong with spending a day stretched out in sweatpants binge-watching your favorites series, unless it becomes a way of life.

Most of us have been there, curling in the nautilus shell of grief and not wanting to move until ... What?

While we wait for some unknown force to propel us back into life, sometimes what little energy we have we waste in self-abuse, berating ourselves with criticism or turning to food, alcohol, or whatever works to numb us further.

What's wrong with me? Ever ask that one? For what it's worth, nothing is wrong with you. You're a survivor who gets to keep on living while a beloved other doesn't. It's a weird place to find yourself, and there's no map.

I'm here to tell you the only force that can move you out of emotional inertia and back into the intentional work of becoming a version of you that knows joy and well-being is, surprise, you. Yes, a tight community of empathetic family and friends and maybe grief support in the form of counseling, psychotherapy, or a group of others dealing with loss can provide a nurturing safety net. Invite those relationships and resources into your mourning if you can.

Ultimately, though, the only one who can really grasp what you are going through is you. You are the only one in your bearish snow cave. The goal is to rouse your sluggish body and murky mind then lead yourself out of the cave, blinking and stretching, into the brightness of the world. If you're more the hurricane-spiraling-fast-to-avoid-your-grief type, the same rituals, habits, and mindsets I'm sharing in this book will help you cool the climate of your hyperactive coping to be more healing.

Are you looking for pearls?

When I think back to that night lying in bed, listening to the owls ask, *Who looks for Purrrrrrrrrlz?* I wonder why I heard the call as that question.

Pearls. They're satiny gems. I have both white pearls I inherited and black pearls from a visit to Fiji. They're mostly layers of calcium crystals made by oysters and muscles. They're a defense mechanism against irritants or invaders, such as parasites, encapsulating them so they can do no harm to the tongue-like and mysterious life form inside the craggy shells.

A pearl starts as a threat and ends as ball of loveliness. Maybe I'm the one looking for pearls, trying to figure out how I can wrap myself around the threat of loss, protect myself, and contain it as a form of beauty.

I don't know how long I listened to the owl couple, but as suddenly as their calls began, they ended. I tipped my head sideways, looking at the silhouette of my husband's sleeping face. I could hear his lungs wheezing, air wrestling with water that shouldn't be there, each breath a small triumph. We don't know when his death will come. Some nights it seems near, and others, gratefully far. *It will be like the owls*, I thought, *this strange music that is his breathing presence, then the sudden silence.*

124

Review:
Stepping Stones to Help You in Your Loss Journey

 Rogue rituals are rituals involving the one we love that may have begun as positive acts or behaviors but in the face of loss take on a disturbing quality or trigger some of grief's darker emotions, such as anger or shame. It helps to identify rogue rituals that may be a roadblock in your mourning process, and release or reframe them.

 Our relationships depend heavily on words, and when the one we love is gone, it's common to regret what was either left unsaid or misunderstood. It helps to look past words to intentions and focus on the love between you.

 Often your loss is shared by others, either in your immediate circle of friends and family or in the form a communal loss affecting many families. Ongoing, living relationships can be damaged when survivors grieve in astonishingly different ways. It helps to aim for compassion and tolerance toward others as well as yourself as you all try to learn how to live with loss, keeping the relationships you have, even if imperfect.

 Sometimes the people most able to offer us support during our grief are not those closest to us. It helps to look beyond immediate, obvious friends and family to others who may be able to offer unconditional nurturing and patience.

Emotional inertia happens when you're stuck either in perpetual motion or languishing in immobility. It can be a major roadblock in moving toward well-being. To get out of emotional inertia requires some force to either pause your motion or ignite you into motion so you can effectively deal with grief and progress through mourning.

 New rituals, habits, and mindsets, even tiny ones, can serve as the force to get you out of your emotional inertia.

9

Sensing

Come back to your senses

When light pours through the window, dust spins, illuminated. You listen for some sound as each fleck spirals its way down, perhaps some singing that moths hear. There is only the music of your breath, that tiny wind, blowing you from one moment into the next.

— from my notebooks, August 2003

Do you taste the world? I know, a strange question. What I want to know is when you move through the day, experiencing whatever is around you, is your first instinct to taste it?

Babies and cats are tasters. They bite and lick and bring small curiosities into their mouths. It's how they try to understand what's in front of them. Wordlessly their tongues seek answers: What is this, is it alive, can you eat it, can you play with it or carry it around like a prize, is it something tasty or nasty?

I've never tasted the pond in my front yard, at least not on purpose, though in pulling out pond weeds, I've certainly managed to get a splashy sample. Now that I think of it, my pond tastes like a combination of moss and dimes, earthy and slightly metallic (don't ask how I know what moss and dimes taste like).

The pond is a fixture in my life that taps all of my senses, especially as I work from my home office that looks out upon it. When I'm not accidentally tasting it, I'll watch it change over the course of the day. The nearly black surface before dawn evolves into shimmers, reflecting light and the feather-weight force of water-striders pushing atop the water. The pond has a distinct decaying, musty smell. Submerging a hand, I'm always surprised how a tree shadow cast across one end of the pond makes the water there chillier than the sunlit water just a few inches away.

The most astounding aspect of the pond, however, is its voice, its sound. Because it's a home to other beings, most notably, Pacific tree frogs and Northern red-legged frogs, the pond can become rowdy. The voices of the frogs, mostly frisky males wanting a mate, sing their frog songs in the night for nearly half the year, a sporadic thrumming that can be heard for miles as well as through a bedroom wall. Some call it noise. To me, it's an earthly lullaby. As I write, the pond is empty of frog music until winter rains come.

Still, many frogs are sneaking around being terrestrial tourists. Chloe kitten encountered one. I was trimming dead fronds from a fern, when I looked up to see Chloe lick something, pick it up in her mouth, delightedly trot a few feet, then drop it. By the time I got to her to see what she'd found, she was frothing at the mouth, profusely, drool dripping from her velvety, confused face. A foamy, thick waterfall spilled from her.

At first, I couldn't see what she'd dropped. Frogs are talented blenders, that is, they blend well into their landscape. Then, I saw an eye wink. A tree frog. Chloe saw the wink, too. Her head, tongue peeking through the foam cloud that was her mouth, jerked toward the frog. With a dead fern frond still in my hand, I gently nudged the green fellow until he hopped safely under a damp redwood log. I grabbed Chloe, who had ambitions of following, and placed her in a soft clump of clover. Soon my frothy kitten was fine. A quick glance at a field guide confirmed that when tree frogs feel threatened, they ooze a coating on their shimmery body that's an emetic, bitter but nontoxic for Chloe. No frog wants to stay long in the mouth of a cat.

I ask again, do you taste the world? Once upon a time, probably yes, you did. Then you learned, as Chloe is still learning, to be judicious about tasting something new. There are other senses for exploring the unknown. No doubt the adults around you also discouraged you from putting anything unusual in your mouth, at least until it was time to introduce Brussel sprouts (I'd rather try the tree frog, thank you very much).

Have you lost your senses?

Unfortunately, as we grow up, we begin to take our senses for granted and may even forget we can intentionally deploy them to deepen our experiences. Our senses are critical to comprehending the environment not only around us, but within us. They help us get out of our head, that thinker part of us. Critical thinking is a Godsend that helps us solve an array of ordinary-to-complex problems, personally and globally. But. Like too much of anything, overthinking can lead us astray, into thought patterns that can be destructive to our well-being.

"I think therefore I am," is an old philosophical concept that still guides the way many define human existence. In that worldview, the fact that we can doubt ourselves is proof we exist. Well, that's a positive basis for life, isn't it? No! I believe it's more accurate to say, "I sense and feel therefore I am," which research in neuroscience increasingly agrees with.

Our senses bring us information and data from the world beyond our bodies as well as from within. That sensory data informs who we are as living beings, who we are in relation to other beings, and who we are as part of the phenomena unfolding (aka stuff happening) around us. As our brains interpret the information delivered through our senses, feelings—both physical and emotional—shape our experience of each moment and influence what we believe about ourselves.

Let's pause for a moment to define our senses. Quick refresher, they are sight, sound, smell, taste, and touch. Our senses are actually more numerous than those, because we also have sensory systems related to the position of our bodies in space, keeping track of our limbs, monitoring temperature, and receiving pain. But for our purposes, we'll focus on those five fundamental senses.

I'd toss in a bonus sixth sense, breath—that great invisible medium that literally draws fragments of the universe inside you and lets you spew back a little of yourself. However, breathing isn't a sense from a scientific standpoint. Breath is that delicate, unseen tide that ties you and the world together physically. It's a miraculous story for another time.

As humans, we rely most heavily on our eyes unless there's a visual impairment. About 80% of our perception of the environment around us comes via sight. There are cultural differences, where some groups or tribes may vary in how much they use certain senses. In most people, though, the visual cortex takes up the largest sensory component of the brain. So, sight is our primary go-to sense.

That said, sight isn't the first sense we use in life. Our first sense is touch.

Afloat inside our mothers at just eight weeks old, looking a bit like a knobby alien, we experience our first sensations in our face. Not much bigger than a tadpole, we're in the early stages of becoming an individual being, our delicate skin containing us while also separating us from all else. Touch is central to distinguishing the self from the other, which in this case is mother. By about 17 weeks and the size of a turnip, we've become more human, with a range of sensations right down to the soles of our teeny feet.

If you think about it, our other four senses are essentially versions of touch. Light touches our retinas. Sound waves touch our ear bones. Scent molecules touch receptors in the cave that's our nose. Taco and cerveza touch our taste buds.

Touch is central to what it means to be human. Touch shapes self-awareness, feeds brain development, and influences behavior. Touch is intimately connected to well-being.

It's no wonder then that the loss of someone we love can be so debilitating. It's not only that we'll never see them again, we'll never touch or be touched by them again. Similarly, it's easy to understand how the shared experience of loss that goes with major events like a COVID-19 pandemic or a civil war in Sierra Leone, which force physical distance between people who love or at least care about each other, leads to deep communal grief.

Hugs and hand-holding are literally healing.

Come back to your senses.

Why am I telling you all of this? It's more than my affinity for the natural history of frogs, cats, and babies. I've learned over the years that the emotional and psychological impacts of loss often make us forget that our senses can help reconnect us to our lives.

What if by paying attention to your senses, for just a few minutes each day, you could take a break from grief and ultimately create space for joy to enter? I'm here to tell you that it does work, at least for me and many others, and my hope is that it will work for you, too.

My life-support system for living with loss emerged out of a period of devastating loss following by my mother's death, Ruth's suicide, and fleeing from one side of the continent to start a new life on the other. I say it emerged because frankly, it was accidental. I was two years trying to claw my way out of a grief hole before I intuitively returned to a simple practice, first in the evening and then added into my mornings, that made all the difference in the world.

I implemented an easy ritual that initially was only a couple minutes a day. I went outside before bedtime, said goodnight to the night, and paid attention to all of my senses, experiencing as fully as possible whatever was unfolding around me. I turned off my thinking mind as much as I could and accepted whatever popped up in my awareness. Then I did the same when I woke up, saying good morning to the morning. I'd be with the morning, my senses wide awake, bringing sensory data into me, making the morning feel like a mystery briefly broken open just for me.

The best analogy I can offer for these morning and evening rituals is slicing open kiwi fruit. A kiwi looks like a drab, furry rock. Who even thought it could be edible? But. Cut it open, and surprise. There's brilliant green flesh and a star of black seeds around a center as if a sun is inside. Once you scoop out a bite and taste it, wow, it's a burst of sweetness and tartness. That's what my tiny sensory rituals did for me with parts of my day.

That simple morning and evening practice amounted to rediscovering a world I'd stopped seeing.

By getting out of my head and letting my body speak to me through my senses, I got relief from grief, even if initially for just a few moments. Having despair, guilt, longing, sorrow, and that oppressive feeling of being overwhelmed lifted for a bit was, as I've shared, like taking off a backpack full of rocks. I literally felt lighter in those moments. Best of all, I realized I could actively make it all happen. I could summon a wave of well-being.

Briefly I could feel that invisible thread of my life within reach. Out of the chaos of loss, such peace. Without trying to control anything other than getting my body outside and shifting my focus from thinking to physically sensing, surprise, I'd taken the reins from grief.

A tiny ritual is a mighty force.

I started calling the nighttime and morning practices my Tiny-Come-Back-to-Your-Senses Rituals.

Usually when people say, come back to your senses, ironically, they're not referring to your senses but to your mind, as in: *Have you lost your mind? What are you thinking? Get your head together, girl. Don't be foolish, come back to your senses!*

Your mind is often the last place you want to be. As you no doubt know, it is so powerful it can drag you into dark places that won't help you thrive. However, the mind is tamable, and its power can be harnessed to help you tackle loss. Mindfully practicing tiny rituals and Joy Habits (another practice you can develop) is transformative.

Remember our exploration of emotional inertia? A thing in motion tends to stay in motion and a thing at rest tends to stay at rest until acted upon by some force. Tiny-Come-Back-to-Your-Senses Rituals are a force to help you either pause your hyperactive frenzy or draw you out of your lethargic bear cave.

Because it's hard to change from action to stillness or from stillness to action, it's best to start any healing ritual as one small step. That step may only create a tiny break from grief initially, but you'll find it's an opening into life, a kind of foot in the door letting in a sliver of light. Once you enter consistently, you'll discover a vastness to that tiny space that will expand. You'll increase the time you spend there. Your relief from grief will grow. Really, no kidding.

As I've shared my Tiny-Come-Back-to-Your-Senses Ritual with others over the years, I've refined the process into a four-step ritual that's implemented initially for only three minutes. The next chapter is dedicated to teaching you that process. You'll begin by focusing on one of your senses, ideally a lesser-used sense, such as smell. Of course, we use our sense of smell all the time—anytime you eat, smell is part of how you experience food. What I mean by lesser-used is that you don't often use it intentionally to explore what's happening around you. It's about taking in all the scents present in a given moment that you usually don't notice.

You can choose any sense to start your tiny sensory ritual. Maybe you want to try tasting the world again, as long as you pay attention to it. If you're not outdoorsy, don't worry, you'll insert your ritual into a routine that isn't broken, which may be part of your indoor life.

Think you don't have time or the stamina to add in even a three-minute Tiny-Come-Back-to-Your-Senses Ritual? I want to challenge your thinking there.

I once shared this concept with a colleague, a high-powered professional. I didn't know her all that well, except that she was pushing herself through a hectic schedule and struggling with the loss of her brother. She swore she was so busy she didn't have time for even a three-minute ritual, and she felt paying attention to her senses sounded too "touchy-feely." At the end of each day, she collapsed into a glass of wine and cried.

She was a gutsy, get-to-the-point, go-getter, so I could be blunt. I asked her, "Do you have time to pee?" She stopped, puzzled, and replied, "Well, yes, I make time for that." "Great." I said, "Then next time, pee and breathe." She looked perplexed. I elaborated, "Next time you pee, pause and spend three minutes just breathing—in, out, in, out, eyes closed. Notice what it feels like to breathe. Pay attention to how miraculous it is that one breath automatically follows another. Just try it a few times and tell me what happens."

A few weeks later, I ran into her. "I thought your idea was too wacky not to try," she said. "I'm desperate to get out of this screw-it-all mode, and now I get it." She was smiling. "The one downside," she continued, "that I guess is an upside, is that the first time I did the pee and breath thing, I was in my own bathroom and picked up a little scent of mildew." She said she ended up cleaning the shower stall. While she didn't always want to be driven to clean, she said doing that tiny breathing ritual sparked a shift in her. "I haven't been motivated to clean anything in months! My condo looks like it's inhabited by a hoard of trolls." She told me her three minutes of just making herself sit and breathe was "this weird breakthrough."

We laughed, and then I went over my four-step tiny ritual process. She decided to create her first Tiny-Come-Back-to-Your-Senses Ritual around what she called her wine time, so she could stop, as she put it, "wrecking a good cabernet with salty tears."

Review:

Stepping Stones to Help You in Your Loss Journey

Tuning into your senses can be a resource for reconnecting you to the world around you and your life.

Paying attention to the sensory input coming into your body helps reduce the over-thinking that often happens as you try to process your loss.

Human beings have many senses, though the five major senses are sight, sound, smell, taste, and touch. We tend to emphasize one or two senses, so spending time focusing on a lesser-used sense can reconnect us to our bodies and the world in new and deeper ways.

The time spent paying attention to your senses, which includes what's happening within your body as well as beyond your body in the world around you, gives you an immediate break from grief while creating an opening for joy to grow.

Successful change is best started with tiny actions. No matter how little time you have or how much emotional inertia you are experiencing, you can create a Tiny-Come-Back-to-Your-Senses Ritual, starting with just three minutes a day.

While breath is not a sense, simply sitting for three minutes focusing on your breath going in and out, rather than on the thoughts zooming through your mind, can bring peace and relief from grief for awhile.

10

Practice

Creating Your Tiny-Come-Back-to-Your-Senses Ritual

Let's explore the broken places in your day.

Before we jump into building a Tiny-Come-Back-to-Your-Senses Ritual, let's explore the shape of your life without the one you love. There are two questions to ask yourself to identify the broken places in your day and how you are coping in those places now.

It's easy to get lost in loss. We often go through the motions of living, hour-to-hour, on automatic pilot—sorrow, disillusionment, longing, or any number of grief emotions blowing through us, rattling us, and pulling us down. We can't avoid some suffering that follows a death (and avoidance isn't the goal), but we don't want prolonged or extreme suffering either.

While the death of someone you love can feel like an explosion that's bigger than the little moments in your day, the reality is, as writer Annie Dillard put it, "How we spend our days is, of course, how we spend we spend our lives." If you don't identify the broken places in your days, it's pretty hard to fix the brokenness in your life.

With a little effort, it's possible to identify what may be triggering difficult feelings or how they're being set loose in the newly dysfunctional parts of your daily or weekly routines.

First, ask yourself this question: How has my life changed on a daily basis because of my loss?

Jot down the three to five ways that your daily life has been most altered now that an important someone is missing. While you could probably make a long list, for our purposes here, focus only on the three to five most compelling impacts you are experiencing daily or almost daily. Focusing on your everyday life is essential.

If you've been a caregiver for the one you lost, a whole group of tasks and chores are no longer needed, and chunks of time are suddenly empty. If you lost a spouse or partner, finding their keys every morning for them or checking in at noon to see how their day is going or feeling frustrated they left the cap off the toothpaste are ordinary moments now lost. Maybe it's your brother who's gone. You didn't see or talk to him very often, but there were points in your day when you thought about him, perhaps forwarding an email about the stupidity of a certain politician or posting a picture of wheat-free lasagna on social media, waiting for one of his quips about gluten-free zombies.

Occasionally, some people have trouble putting their finger exactly on how their day has become broken. Try walking through a typical day before your loss from the time you woke up until you tucked yourself in at night. Then look at that typical day now. It's important, really it is, to identify where key points in your day don't work the same way, or at all.

Second, ask this question: How am I filling the changed moments or empty spaces in my day now?

Once you have your three to five impacts or broken places in your day, I want you to think about how you are filling those gaps. Again, if you were a caregiver and you no longer need to give care, what are you doing in the spaces when you used to tend to your loved one? If you touched base by phone with your husband or daughter every day at noon, what fills the time where those conversations used to be?

Sometimes the space just fills with random busyness, other times you find yourself sobbing and falling into deepening despair, and still other times maybe you've established a new, healing outlet to fill those times, like going for a walk or connecting with a friend.

Your answers to these questions will show you where your daily routine is broken as well as where you have already built new rituals and habits that may or may not be contributing to your well-being. Once you have been practicing your Tiny-Come-Back-to-Your-Senses Ritual and implement a Joy Habit (which we'll discuss in the next section), you'll be introducing them into the broken places where you're feeling stuck or anxious or engaging in less-than-ideal coping strategies. So, save your list.

Let's identify what's still working.

Keeping those answers in mind, now ask yourself: Where in my day is my routine working well? In establishing any new ritual or habit, you want to build on what's working in a consistent, healthy way.

My initial Tiny-Come-Back-to-Your-Senses Rituals were built into the ending and then the beginning of each day. Now I have several tiny sensory rituals throughout the day. My first was a nighttime ritual. Before bed, I had a routine of checking all of the doors to make sure they were locked. Regardless of how well or poorly I was handling my losses, I always checked those doors. It was easy to add in a ritual of stepping out of the backdoor to stand on the deck or wander further out to the riverbank, when I lived along a river. Then all had to do was use my senses to see what was going on in the environment around me, which made me feel part of it, alive, and usually grief-free for a bit. Often, I'd send good intentions out to people I was holding in my thoughts for whatever reason, my version of prayer. I'd conclude by saying goodnight to the night, looking up at whatever was there, stars or moon or purple-black clouds. Finally, I'd wonder back inside, lock that last door, and head off to bed.

What I want you to do today—and there's no better time to start than immediately after finishing this chapter—is begin your Tiny-Come-Back-to-Your-Senses Ritual by taking two actions:

- First, pick a time in your day where you've determined you have a consistent working routine that you can add to.

- Second, spend three minutes, just three little minutes, using at least one sense you don't normally use.

Eventually I encourage you to use multiple senses, but let's start with at least one, lesser-used sense to take a break from any sadness, regret, loneliness, anxiety, fatigue—whatever your feelings of loss look like today. Once you've given this practice a try, you can then add this new Tiny-Come-Back-to-Your-Senses Ritual into the place in your daily routine that's functioning, piggybacking your ritual onto existing habits.

Again, if you are in the early raw-grief stage of your loss where you're unable to focus attention on your senses or they have the potential to trigger more pain than relief, then wait until you are further along on your loss journey.

For some, it helps to have a way to time the ritual. If you have an old-fashioned three-minute egg timer, great, grab it, or you can set a digital timer or alarm—just nothing obnoxious that would rattle you at the end of your three minutes. For this practice, I recommend against your smartphone. This three minutes needs to be as distraction-free as possible, and smartphones are really dumb when it comes to not distracting you.

Here's the process:

There are Four Steps to your Tiny-Come-Back-to-Your-Senses Ritual. Let me list them first, and then we'll go over each step:

- **Step 1:** Check in with your emotions. Name how you are feeling in the moment, and say it or whisper it out loud

- **Step 2:** Check in with your body, paying attention to the sensations of each body part, starting at your toes and moving up inside your body to the crown of your head.

- **Step 3:** Focus on a lesser-used sense and what it brings to you for three minutes. If you're focusing on smell, what scents and aromas reach your awareness? If it's sound, what do you hear—near then far, loud then soft as can be? Stay in this step for at least three minutes.

- **Step 4:** Check out with your emotions and body. How do you feel emotionally and physically? Any change from the emotion you named in step one? Any physical, sensory changes—muscles more relaxed, forehead less tense?

Here's the step-by-step practice.

The first day or week of starting this practice, you may focus entirely on the first two steps, your mood and body check-ins, for the full three minutes. We're often disconnected emotionally and especially physically from our own bodies. After awhile, you'll move through these two check-ins pretty quickly and will focus almost all of your three minutes on step three, coming back to your senses.

Step 1: Check-In With Your Emotions. Take a moment to acknowledge how you're feeling emotionally. Maybe you're feeling fear or numb, or maybe you realize you're feeling pretty upbeat. Whatever you are feeling emotionally, name it and say it out loud or whisper it to yourself. I feel exhausted or I feel regret or I feel hopeful—whatever it is for you in that moment. You're simply assessing and acknowledging where you are at the start of your tiny ritual. Then speak your Feeling Intent: "I want to feel _____ (whatever feeling you chose in the first Practice session)."

Step 2: Check-In With Your Body. Give your attention to how your body feels, each individual part, as if your body is a community of separate beings. Start at your feet and climb up through your body to the crown of your head—toes to knees to belly to ribs to elbows to ear lobes. When I do it, I often feel like a little monkey climbing up inside a tree checking out all of the branches and leaves.

Closing your eyes usually works best to be able to focus on each body part and the sensation of that body part. For instance, paying attention to your big toe on your left foot, what is it feeling? Is it cold against the floor, warm and cozy in a slipper, itchy in a wool sock, a little numb? Rising up through your ankles then calves, what do they feel? Muscles tense or relaxed, achy or energized? When you reach your gut and abdomen, what's going on there? Gurgling? Soft or knotted? Keep rising up in your body, letting each part tell you whatever it needs to tell you. Pay special attention to your face. Are you smiling? Is your forehead or that space behind your eyes taut or at ease? Any part of you feel especially hot or cold inside?

You don't need to summarize all of the sensations into a single assessment as you did with your emotions. Simply recognizing how your body's members are each experiencing the moment with you is enough. (See the beginning of this book to download a **free** copy of the **Grieving Us** audiobook, which includes more detailed audio guidance for this step.)

Step 3: Focus on One of Your Senses. After your check-ins, you pick one of your senses to focus on for at least three minutes. I suggest selecting one of your lesser-used senses, because it can open up the moment in different ways than you are used to when, for instance, you are mostly paying attention to what you see. Let's say you focus on your sense of smell. My kittens live in the world of smell, but human beings tend to pay it little attention unless the pungent arrival of a skunk or the sting of a potent onion slams the sensory neurons inside our noses.

Smell is a good sense to play with because it's also connected to breath, and mindfully breathing is so good for you. Our sense of smell can also be a positive trigger for memories, beautiful memories. That said, if a scent is likely to trigger negative or hurtful memories, then select taste or hearing. Ideally, make sure the new rituals you are starting are distinct and separate from the loved one you've lost and the rituals associated with them. If your loved one was into aroma therapy, again, think carefully about whether focusing on your sense of smell makes sense at this point. This ritual could make you feel close to them and comforted, or it could remind you how much you miss them and amplify your grief.

For your tiny ritual, you can stand or sit or lie down, though try not to fall asleep. Start your three-minute timer. With your eyes open, breathe in through your nostrils. What do you notice when you breathe in? What scents do you pick up? Breathe out. Can you smell when you're exhaling? Close your eyes, and breathe in again, what's that like? What scents do you pick up? Pleasant? Musty? Perfumed from your soap or shampoo? The litter box in the other room? Last night's salmon? Something else vague and unnamable? Is your sense of smell stronger with your eyes open or closed?

As you focus on smell, you may find other senses speaking to you, like the sound of your breath in and out of your nostrils, or maybe you catch a little breeze as your exhalations touch your upper lip. Pay attention to your sense of smell and be open to whatever else happens. Play! Inhale deeply or just shallow. Exhale slow or with a big huff at the end. Breathe normally but really try to savor the air and notice subtle aromas.

By the way, you might try practicing this sensory component of your ritual at different times of the day and inside versus outside. The first time I tried using my sense of smell, outdoors on my deck, just before sunrise, I was surprised beyond belief at how rich the world smelled—the dewy railing, the damp leaves and earth, the morning mist thick on the air I was inhaling. There was this overall earthy, wet, alive aroma, as well as individual scents or tiny currents coming into me and my awareness. Pretty cool actually. I still start every morning with this practice.

Step 4: Check Out. When your egg-timer runs out of sand, starts to chime, or however you know you've been practicing this ritual for at least three minutes, do a single emotional and physical check-out on how you are feeling overall. Do you sense any shift, even subtly, in how you feel now? If you were anxious at the start—or whatever you named your emotion in Step One—are you a little calmer? If your shoulders were tense at the start, how are they now? Did you get a break from grief during your three-minute Tiny-Come-Back-to-Your-Senses Ritual?

For some, the attempt at a tiny ritual brings surprisingly meaningful relief that lasts long after their three minutes. For others, the initial impact is mild, but enough they can see that with practice, reconnecting with their lives is possible. A few say they felt silly, wondering if this process is a waste.

If you fall into the last category, it's usually because your mind was too busy, focused more on intellectually thinking and judging rather than simply paying attention to your senses. With this practice, you want to be mindful of your senses but not in your mind, thinking too much. The irony is that this practice is the very thing that can help tame your overthinking mind and let your body communicate with, and reconnect you to, the world and to your life. Regardless, a ritual isn't a one and done deal. The very meaning of ritual is an act, or series of acts, that are repeated consistently. So, don't give up. Try another sense and see if that works better for you.

Let's integrate your tiny sensory ritual.

Once you've determined which sense you want to start with and understand the process, it becomes a ritual by adding it into your daily routine intentionally. You're going to find some spot in your day where there is some semblance of a consistent routine. Mornings are often the most routine-oriented. There's also the added value that a morning ritual can set the tone for the rest of the day. If you're not a morning person, don't try to make yourself change, at least not until you're feeling more grounded. Instead, find a point in your day tied to a routine you typically follow no matter what and that makes the most sense for you. Maybe it's right after lunch or that transitional space as you move from workday to evening.

While I started my own sensory ritual process just before bed, when it was time to lock all the doors, it's my morning ritual that I find most helpful in setting the stage for well-being. I piggybacked on to making my first cup of tea. Regardless of how much emotional inertia I might be experiencing, I always make that morning cup of tea, so it was easy to just "add on" a tiny ritual.

The tea-making was my trigger. Cup in hand, I started a ritual of stepping out onto the deck and just standing there. First, I sniffed the tea— wow, chai, the cinnamon and clove, all so fragrant! I watched the steam rise into the air and disappear, magical. I felt the heat of the cup in my hand. I sipped the tea and paid attention to how it tasted, how scent and taste work together, then the warmth sliding over my tongue and down through my throat. I listened. I discovered, the very first time I truly paid attention, that simply opening the door and stepping out into a still-dark morning felt more like entering rather than exiting. It wasn't stepping out of the house, I was stepping into something. I'm not sure I can adequately name it, but into a big limitless space, rich and layered and wild.

The morning smelled differently than the rest of the day. It sounded unique, with its own subtle music of distant cars, the hum of all the motors that run a human world as well as hidden birds rustling leaves, a faraway dog howling then yipping, last night's rain dripping into the mud. You get the idea?

Now I have multiple tiny rituals imbedded in the routines that move me through my day. The key is to connect your Tiny-Come-Back-to-Your-Senses Ritual with a part of your daily routine that's still intact. Later you'll extend your tiny ritual beyond three minutes, then add an intentional Joy Habit. Eventually, you may move your ritual and habit, or create new ones, to fill or bridge those broken places you identified in your day. For now, just focus on practicing your sensory ritual consistently, as a path toward your Feeling Intention.

Section 3

Rebuilding your life by doing what you love

11

Cultivating

Well-being and joy are growable

We forget to be grateful for skin, how it holds us together so we don't spill ourselves on the sidewalk or leave our hearts on a park bench. It hides all the mess inside, along with the emptiness tunneling through. It lets us walk through the world as beings constantly touched and touching, the first threshold for joy.
— from my notebooks, September 2014

Paddling in thick, cold fog just after dawn, I wondered, *Is this what Pablo entered or what he left behind?* I was on Big Lagoon, which edges the Pacific Ocean. I could barely see to either end of my kayak, but I kept gliding forward. The fog made the visible world small, but also the unseeable oddly palpable and more real.

There was a bar of sand between me and open ocean, which is what defines the lagoon, three-and-a-half-miles long. I paddled parallel to it. A tawny smudge in the fog at the corner of my eye, the bar allowed me the comfortable illusion that I was contained within boundaries, the sand wall keeping me from being swept out to sea, and my own body keeping me in this life.

It was New Year's Day, 2014. I remember thinking, *I'm here. Pablo is not.* That's loss in its simplest terms. Only 36, he died suddenly on Christmas night. Like everyone who loved Pablo, I was stunned. How did a day of giving turn into a night of inconceivable taking? I spoke his name. "Pablo." It came out as fog blending with fog. Then I thought, *He is here, by the mere saying of his name, Pablo.*

A loon let loose his eerie song, a tangled arc of shrill tones. He was invisible, existing in the murky, wet air only as music. I didn't need to see him to believe in him. The mind likes its connections, so the song reminded me Pablo was a musician, too. The loon called again, as if expecting an answer that never came. "Namaste," I whispered, wondering if he heard me, the loon, that is, but also Pablo.

Tiny beads of water hung from my eye lashes. If I looked straight up, they become strange lenses. It was the fog clinging and pooling on those tiny curls of hair. Then I added to them with my own tears. Humans are such a liquid lifeform, 70% water. I was a wet being emerged in a wet world, so little separating what is alive from what is not. For a moment I felt so incredibly sad because Pablo was gone, and then, surprise, I felt joy.

A bright white stain spread radially in one spot of the sky. It was the sun, muted. It felt good to know it was still out there doing its fusion, 600 billion tons of hydrogen turned helium every half a breath or so. Atoms were colliding and merging, giving light and heat. I was there to see it, glowing proof that the universe and I were both okay.

Every human, and all that is not human, is a sack of recycled sun. We are made out of used atoms and star parts. No one is ever really lost, just rearranged.

That morning at the put-in, a river otter was waiting. She looked like a dripping comma on the bank of the lagoon. She watched as I launched my gaudy, orange 'yak, bumbling about in the near dark. As I drifted away, she stood up in the mud, slipping to water like a sliver of time, all silk and glitter, quick and gone.

Later out on the lagoon enveloped in mist, thinking of Pablo and the submerged sun, feeling like the only person alive, I saw a subtle waking of the water coming toward me. There was bubbling, then stillness. Excited, I whispered to myself, "She's followed me!" I paddled as gently as I could, barely stirring the surface. I thought, as I always do when I want to see a bird or animal, *Let me see you, please*, half-believing in mental telepathy or a creature's ability to sense good intentions.

The water rippled again, a path of bubbles coming toward me and disappearing beneath me. *She went under my boat!* The water went slack and almost black. Then it happened again, the otter inside in a ridge of water approaching, a living torpedo, the bubbles of her breathing pres-ence slipping under my kayak then popping up on the other side. Her shimmering, whiskered face, like a wet, wide-faced dog, bobbed at the water's surface so close I could touch her, but didn't. I froze, as we looked at each other. *Memorize her!*

There were droplets suspended from her eyelashes. The oily fur on her forehead was neatly combed into rows thanks to the force of pushing her face through the lagoon. Her whiskers were a wild mustache, each wiry strand strung with pearls of water. I breathed in her musky scent, a combo of algae and sweaty socks. I couldn't see the small slips of her ears, which were below the surface, so I hummed low. She tipped her head sideways, making one loud chirp like a bird. Who knew an otter speaks in chirps?

What did she make of me? Our eyes connected for what seemed like an eternity but also quick as a wink. We existed in a rare moment outside of time. Finally, she dropped into the oblivion of the lagoon.

I felt such well-being, peace, and belonging, even love, as foolish as that may sound. I connected to something bigger than me. What? I can't say—only that it added up to joy.

I looked hard through the fog for her and stared into the lagoon. *She's gone.* The water was a near-perfect mirror, reflecting what was above it—a woman with a colorful knit hat and blue-green eyes, blinking at herself.

How often do we look at the "other" and see the impenetrable, or worse, only ourselves?

We're so good at projecting ourselves on others, stuck in our *idea* of them, that sometimes we miss discovering who they really are. I knew Pablo only a bit better than Ms. Otter. The only son of dear friends, Pablo has been gone years as I recall this memory now. Hard to believe so much time has elapsed.

Have you ever had that experience, the disorienting unease of realizing that the world and you have moved forward and left someone important behind?

Memory's job is to recalibrate time, connecting past to present. Thanks to memories, the one you love and lost gets to join you, a stowaway on your journey. It can never be the same as their physical being, but at some point, you take what you can get.

I try to conjure Pablo's face, but beyond a lighter version of his father's curly hair, I can't without pulling photos of him from the side of the refrigerator. There he is blowing on a melodica and there with his steelpan drums.

Oddly, I can still play his voice in my head, talking about his two little dogs, Apple and Peanut, and his fiancé singing opera. He's telling me how far she travels, how he waits for her to come home, and how long the waiting feels. Somehow, I've carried his longing for his sweetheart. No, I didn't know Pablo well, but I feel in my hollowing, osteopenic bones how much he loved his opera singer and their two dachshunds and being a music maker.

Perhaps we never really know people, but sense them, like a form of gravity grounding us or a tidal force shifting inside us and through us.

That New Year's morning, almost a week without Pablo, I sat for a long time in the quiet of winter water birds. A Pied-billed grebe kept diving and bobbing up. Buffleheads, the sleek black males with their white wedge-y heads, would flap then run atop the water to lift away from me. Traffic on the hidden highway occasionally broke through the fog and my attention. Then I'd noticed the ocean on the other side of the sand bar, its stamping and applause of surf. I waited for the otter to reappear, listening to the synthetic rubbing of my life jacket as it followed my breathing in and out. Ms. Otter wasn't coming back. Pablo was still dead. My sadness remained. But. I felt joy. How could that be?

There's happy, and then there's real joy.

Joy is a habit. Like love, joy can be cultivated and practiced until it grows into a habit. Joy is more than feeling good—it's a form of resilience that helps you endure having your life broken so you can remake it.

If you're struggling with feelings of loss, grief, sadness, maybe hopelessness or a touch of desolation, you might think how can someone be happy when they're experiencing pain?

Happy and joy are related words, but they're different. Happiness is typically triggered by something outside of us, an experience. That's why we tend to say something "made" us happy. Riding on a rollercoaster makes me happy, and the memory of it makes me happy, so long as the person next to me doesn't get nauseated (that makes for a bad experience and a strange memory). Feeling happy is wonderful! It's also fleeting until the next thing that "makes" you happy.

Joy is an inside job. It grows out of feeling connected to your own life. It's a sense of belonging to this world and this moment, to this place in time and space that is your physical, emotional, mental, and spiritual life. It encompasses peace and well-being. Joy is intuitively knowing you are meant to be here, that you matter.

Seeing the otter swirl about my kayak, looking into her otter face made me happy in the surprise and rarity of the experience. But there was more to it than fleeting happiness. The joy came from inside, and it lingered. I was actively part of that surprise and rarity. Active is a key differentiator of joy versus passively riding through the moment on a rollercoaster.

Let me clarify. I wasn't actively summoning joy in the midst of grief. Instead, I was activating a few of my Tiny-Come-Back-to-Your-Senses Rituals, which created a break in the sadness for joy to emerge alongside it. I interacted with Ms. Otter, paying attention to the details of her as an individual. I deployed multiple senses, short of licking and petting her, which I doubt she'd have appreciated (did I tell you about her healthy, canine teeth?). I saw her, I smelled her, I drew a sound from her. Curious, we both leaned into the moment, fully alive.

I share this story of Pablo and the otter because it's an example of how my life-support system for living with loss worked for me on that early New Year's Day. I was mourning for Pablo's sudden disappearance from the world, paddling through grief as dense as the fog. At the same time,

160

by turning to my tiny sensory rituals that I'd been practicing for years at that point, joy happened.

Joy is always hanging out, even if it takes the form of a shadow or the sliver of a shadow in the midst of grief. Long after I came to believe in that shadow, that possibility of joy existing, ever-present, almost waiting for me regardless of what was going on in my life, I found I couldn't make joy happen. It took integrating my Tiny-Come-Back-to-Your-Senses Rituals into my daily routine and then adding in what I call Joy Habits as part of those rituals.

Tiny sensory rituals pause your despair, serve as a subtle force to intervene in your emotional inertia, and open space for doing something that has the potential to bring you joy. With consistent practice, joy becomes a habit.

In the next two chapters, I'll explain what I mean when I talk about a Joy Habit. Then in the Practice chapter, I'll help you create a Joy Habit that you will add on to your Tiny-Come-Back-to-Your-Senses Ritual when you're ready.

Keep on paddling.

I don't remember how long I stayed on Big Lagoon, probably a few hours. A friend at the time asked me if I got lost in the fog that day or if I was afraid, being alone out there. No, physically I had my bearings. The ocean roared like another wild animal on the other side of that long sand bar, so I always knew where I was. Ms. Otter, the loon, all the waterbirds, even the fog and the water beneath by boat reminded me that we're never really alone. If anything, all that wet, dense grey felt like an escape away from the world of humans and loss, safe and protected for awhile.

Emotionally, yes, I was lost a bit. Remember what I said earlier? To grieve one death is always to grieve our own. Impolite to admit, but we weep as much for ourselves, for our very temporary selves, as we do for the people we lose along the way.

Kayaking is one of my periodic Joy Habits. Paddling is a form of meditation for me. The physical act of moving my paddle through air and water can take me out of my over-thinking head and focus my attention on being fully immersed in the moment. To propel my crazy, too-orange kayak across Big Lagoon is to push and pull simultaneously. One paddle edge is coaxed through water while the other vaults through air.

Remembering Pablo that morning, as I paddled away from the muddy put-in, I thought, *Now the dark depth of loss*, as one end of my paddle dipped into the lagoon. Then as the other end of the paddle rose toward sky, I thought, *Now the bright possibility of living.* I'm a poet, so yes, I actually thought those phrases. You're a poet in your mind, before words spill out on a page. The alternating rhythm of the paddle and of those opposite ideas were how I actively mourned.

If you've never paddled a kayak, let me explain a detail. Each time, just before you tip the paddle to break the water's surface, there is a subtle pause, and ever-so-briefly the paddle is suspended between watery earth and sky. What I've come to realize is that pause, where all movement is suspended, is so like being in the limbo of loss before we've found our way through grief to joy. When we're suspended between what was and what can be, the only way out of that limbo is to keep paddling.

Review:
Stepping Stones to Help You in Your Loss Journey

Joy is available to you even in the midst of grief. Opening up your senses, paying attention to the world around you, and doing something that supports your well-being creates openings for joy to emerge within you.

Sometimes you see others through a filter, through your idea of who they are or even projecting your feelings and emotions on them. In losing someone you love, it helps to remember some of the details that were unique to them as a way of holding them in your life.

You aren't as separate from others as you may think. Remembering that you are made out of the stuff of the universe, at a physical level, can help you feel more connected to your loved one as still being in the universe albeit in a different form.

Happy and joy are related words, but they're different. Happiness is typically triggered by something outside of you, an experience. Joy is an inside job. It grows out of feeling connected to your own life.

Joy is more than feeling good—it's a form of resilience that helps you endure having your life broken so you can remake it.

Doing a physical activity, a Joy Habit, can help you align and work through what's happening with you emotionally, mentally, and spiritually.

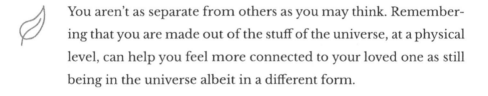

12

Acting

Your life deepens by doing

You wobble between losing and lost, that pair of pockets with holes, as if your life has become little more than worn trousers. You don't want to move, each step the possibility of more slipping away. But what else can you do with those feet? They want to walk—they need to do what they were meant to do.

— from my notebooks, June 2019

There are nearly eight billion people in the world. How many of them do you know?

Let's face it, each of us lives among strangers, and when we leave the planet, we will leave a vast community, a home, we barely know. I didn't realize it at the time, but that's why I traveled to Sierra Leone in late 2013.

165

Who are these others I'll otherwise never know? I arrived eight months or so before an Ebola outbreak and 11 years after a brutal war that took more than 50,000 lives.

On the surface, I travelled to Sierra Leone as part of my work as a fundraiser for a humanitarian organization. It was about visiting villages to see how charitable funding fueled community development projects—a hand-pumped well here, a health hut there, children learning to read, and all those latrines, sadly, too hot, dark, and snaky to use. A donor myself, I'd funded the building of a humble, very rural two-room school in memory of my parents with a modest inheritance. I wanted to see the school and to meet the two children I sponsored there.

Below the surface, after a series of deep losses that lingered, knocking my sense of place in this world off-kilter, I made the journey as part escape, part search. Waves, that's how you lose relationships sometimes, in waves, and before long, there's no place for your feet to touch down.

In the absence of those I loved, I wanted others to care about. It's not that I didn't have plenty of people and animals in my life to love. I loved and was loved. One of the curiosities of loss is that it can open the door to giving more love.

Still, I knew my grief was nothing special, so why not take it to Sierra Leone? Learn. After a ravaging 11-year war, I could imagine how unrelenting, and communal, grief may be. There'd be no escaping the daily reminders of knobbed wrists where hands used to be and cheeks, a landscape of scars. Preparing for my trip, I watched a video clip about postwar life not expecting the images of people doing ordinary things.

How, I wondered, *does grief become resilience, become women preparing rice, laughing?*

I entered Sierra Leone via Liberia through palm oil plantations and an arm of the Gola Rainforest. I travelled with two Sierra Leone colleagues from Freetown, Fataba and Osman. We drove and drove and drove. There

166

were few paved roads then, so Osman, who handled the driving, mostly steered along slippery ruts in the red-clay earth typically travelled by foot or motorbikes. We got stuck in soupy, rust-colored mud more than once.

After a few long days, I realized that Fataba was quietly singing a familiar song. Fataba was the Sierra Leone program director for the international organization we both worked for. The best part of my time in her country was getting to know her. She spoke multiple tribal languages, along with Krio (like Creole) and a British English tinged with the bubbling inflections of her own native Mende.

As we bumped and lunged along, the Land Cruiser more like a struggling pack animal than a vehicle, her voice rose. Sitting in the backseat behind Fataba, I was following her intricate braids, her hair woven into an elaborate, artistic creation, when her words caught me, "Take me home . . . country roads . . . to the place . . . I belong . . . West Virginia . . . Mountain Mama . . . take me home . . . country roads."

She was singing John Denver's song, "Take Me Home, Country Roads."

I started singing along, our voices swelling to full volume, mingling, merging, filling the vehicle. Osman glanced at me in the rearview mirror, his eyes pleased. A quiet, gracious man descended from an esteemed Fula chief (think royalty), he never seemed wearied by the rough driving, always offering his hand, suede-soft, to help me in and out of that backseat. Our reflections looking at each other, he grinned and nodded as Fataba and I sang and sang.

Then I asked Fataba how in the world she came to know that American song, and she shared a story, part of her Loss Story. She was a young woman when the rebels went mad in her country, looting and burning villages, hacking people with machetes, cutlasses as she called them, and abducting children, the boys to be beaten and drugged into soldiers, the girls for sexual exploitation. Her family fled to Guinea where they were sheltered with other refugees by a Catholic priest.

Each morning the priest played that song, John Denver's voice joined by the refugees' voices, ringing out into the sultry West African air. As she spoke, I thought, *John Denver surely would have loved the solace those refugees found in his lyrics.* He couldn't have envisioned the power of his song to bring together displaced people in such a faraway place, let alone how his song would connect two women from different cultures in a 4 x4 in the middle of a rainforest.

"We wanted to return to our homes where we belonged on our country roads," Fataba explained of her time as a refugee. "The song gave us faith." I could see that. I could see the song took them home before peace did.

The priest had the wisdom to understand that people far from home, people whose lives were truly shattered, needed more than food, shelter, and safety. To help them through the limbo of war and displacement, he realized they needed faith and some semblance of routine. They needed temporary rituals and habits, new stepping stones to get them through their days in his care.

Music, which had been a meaningful dimension of most refugee's former lives, had fallen away as communities were disrupted by violence and then the need to quietly slip out of Sierra Leone. Fataba shared how at first it was "difficult to sing when you are sad." She explained how singing was like finding her voice, as if the war had taken that away, too, and she was reclaiming it. Her new refugee ritual brought more than faith that she would return to Sierra Leone someday, it was a way to cultivate joy in the midst of unimaginable loss.

With daily repetition, singing that song ultimately became a habit. After she returned to her country to remake her life, she kept singing, all kinds of songs. In learning to live with her losses, Fataba had become someone who sings. She broke into singing "Take Me Home, Country Roads" whenever she wanted to comfort herself. That day in the Land Cruiser, it wasn't just me away from my family. Fataba and Osman were away from their families, too. As the trip wore on, Fataba couldn't help being a little home-sick. Singing that unlikely John Denver song made us kindred spirits in our longing for home and family.

You can cultivate joy in the midst of loss.

Have you ever had that experience after a loss when something suddenly made you laugh, and then you caught yourself and stopped? I'm talking about that internal critic that barks, *How can you be happy, even for an instant, when death has visited and taken away someone you love?*

I believe we are meant to live with joy and our bodies know it. Even in the aftermath of loss, being a whole person means balancing tears with laughter. Indeed, the word healing evolved from a Latin word meaning "to make whole."

When we're grieving, we often shut out anything that might make us happy, and we close off the internal space in ourselves where joy might take root. When we shutdown joy and block happiness, however, we're reinforcing a negative experience—suffering.

Suffering is a response to what happens to us and within us. We can suffer on all levels of our life—physically, emotionally, mentally, and spiritually—sometimes all at the same time. With certain forms of suffering, but not all, we'll find we have no or minimal ability to control or avoid it. Suffering is an inherent, if unpleasant, part of living. But. Left unopposed, suffering turns into a way of life.

Suffering can become a corrosive habit without Joy Habits to counterbalance it. Worse, the longer we stay in suffering, the harder it will be to know joy again.

Why? Our animal brains like what's known and familiar, convincing our human minds to stay put and help maintain what's perceived as normal and predictable. As we stall in suffering, while it may be painful, we know what that pain is. Creating a new life, trying to introduce new rituals and habits, and inviting joy to come stay for awhile, is moving into the unknown. The brain and mind resist boldly going where we haven't been before or in a long time.

Did you know that your habits are more than just behaviors or a mindset? When unrelenting grief, stress, anxiety, and other forms of emotional suffering become habitual, they actually change the way your body works, affecting all of the systems that keep you alive. Your immune system weakens leaving you susceptible to diseases. Your gut becomes irritable to the point you may not even absorb enough nutrition from your food. Your brain and nervous system short-circuit. Your heart can literally be broken, beating irregularly, causing chest pain and respiratory distress, even progressing to permanent damage or heart attack.

Compare that to laughing, or like Fataba, singing a song. Both laughter and singing are cardiovascular activities that make your heart beat stronger and your lungs breath more deeply, delivering more oxygen to your cells, which can be oxygen-thirsty with long-term suffering. When you laugh or sing, science has shown that your immune system is positively stimulated, making you more resistant to viruses, bacterial infections, and even cancer. Like an all-in-one miracle tonic, laughing and singing benefit you at the physical, emotional, mental, and spiritual levels.

Best of all, when you laugh or sing, your body releases endorphins. Endorphins are neurochemical analgesics, in other words, they are the body's natural pain relievers and pleasure enhancers. Before you grab that glass of wine, a beer, or a bit of marijuana, try a little laughing and singing.

Moving beyond a smile and a song.

What do these have in common? Beekeeping, hiking, podcasting, biking, shooting hoops, kombucha making, photography, dog training, sculpting, meditation, weightlifting, rock hunting, running, quilting, fly tying, painting, composting, yoga, vegetable gardening, bench building, putting, coloring, stargazing, guitar playing, swimming, songwriting, dancing, slacklining, collecting driftwood, bread baking, tutoring, letter-writing to prisoners, recycling, hair braiding, goat raising, programming robots, online selling, cheesemaking, genealogy, jewelry design, video creation, journaling, woodcarving, and I could go on.

If you guessed hobbies, well, sort of, though there's more to it. These are all Joy Habits practiced by the amazing diversity of people I've known in my personal life or encountered in my professional work over the years as a charitable giving and end-of-life planner and nonprofit leader.

While each of these activities has a different way of impacting our well-being, the fact is engaging in any regular activity that enables you to experience joy even for a few minutes most days is grounding. Like laughing and singing, establishing a habit of doing something you love has real, and sometimes profound, impacts on your physical, emotional, mental, and spiritual health. Your blood pressure, heart rate, stress hormones such as cortisol and adrenaline, breathing, gut function, and an array of biochemical, neurotransmitter, and other life-supporting bodily systems are positively affected.

While not a cure for grief, anxiety, depression, and loneliness, Joy Habits are a counterbalance. They give you a break from all of those draining emotions and moods, and they stimulate healing on so many levels. That healing is a form of strength, a resilience, that better equips you to limit your time in pain. By mindfully practicing one, or more, Joy Habits, well-being will inhabit more and more of your life. Let me be clear here, I'm not just talking about while you are practicing your Joy Habit—the effect is far greater—this type of habit has a lingering effect that will flow over into the rest of your life.

The formula for a Joy Habit is simple: **Actively Doing + Regularly Doing + Cultivating Joy = Well-being.**

Zoning out in front of the telly every night is regular but typically passive and doesn't bring joy. Maybe you're binging on sitcoms, and laughing, which is good for you, and does provide grief relief. But. That's a fleeting, make-you-happy experience rather than a long-term joy builder.

Remember, joy is an inside job. It grows out of feeling connected to your own life. It's a sense of belonging to this world and this moment, to this place in time and space that is your physical, emotional, mental, and spiritual life. It encompasses peace and well-being. Joy is intuitively knowing you are meant to be here, that you matter. As much as I enjoy watching *Seinfeld* and Robin Williams Stand-Up Comedy reruns, I can't say when I finally turn off the telly that I feel joy.

Of course, there are exceptions, and that's where the formula helps distinguish between a habit that functions as a diversion, or temporary escape from grief, versus a habit that's cultivating long-term joy in your life every day.

For instance, let's keep that telly turned on. When my father's COPD was so severe at the end of his life that he couldn't do much of anything he enjoyed, classic moving-watching became his Joy Habit. It started as a make-you-happy distraction in the early days of grieving my mother, then it evolved.

He made a science out of picking old musicals, reorganizing his own computer database for tracking them, learning the backstory on each of his favorite movies with the help of Yahoo, and analyzing dance styles. If you wanted to see my father get really animated, try debating him on whether Fred Astaire or Gene Kelly was a better dancer then listen as he explained the virtues of grace versus athleticism. The musicals revived an old dream of being a singer and dancer himself.

His engineer mind would never have called movie-watching a Joy Habit, nor would he have described how the musicals brought greater peace and well-being and made him feel more deeply connected to his life. All I can say is I witnessed it, how those happy-ending, song-and-dance movies were his Joy Habit. They not only brought 90 or 120 minutes of relief from grief, the joy lingered through his days, and though his health could only decline due to his disease, his spirit was resilient.

If you're not a couch potato heading for the remote control at the end of the day, perhaps you're powering through work emails until midnight. That's typically not a Joy Habit either. It may be active and something you do regularly, though more likely it's just a useful way to block the emptiness that can haunt us by evening time when we're struggling with loss. When people ask what you did last night that was fun, do you respond by describing the joy you experienced responding to your boss's emails? It's certainly possible, but I'm guessing, no.

Look at the formula again: **Actively Doing + Regularly Doing + Cultivating Joy = Well-being**. Almost anything can be your Joy Habit if it lives up to that formula.

Does pouring through your emails, perhaps with a side of Internet surfing, qualify as a Joy Habit? Sorry, typically NOT. That said, we are each unique in how we mourn and in what nurtures joy within us. We can surprise ourselves at times, too. For instance, there is one brief exception for me where dealing with email led to joy. It grew out of my work with charitable donors, which involves lots of email exchanges.

One donor in his late 80s was grappling with a terminal illness and the rollercoaster of hope. He kept being offered long-shot treatments that only took away more quality of life, and he was on the downward slope. Still, he had a plucky sense of humor and reveled in posing philosophical questions that we explored over long emails dialogues. I felt joy, not in sitting in front of a monitor, tapping keys, but in the deepening of the relationship with this one-of-a-kind individual I got to know from the inside out. Our emails weren't business-as-usual—they were little works of art full of humanity

Beginning as a ritual, deep with intention, this process became a brief Joy Habit, maybe four or five months. I actively scanned my email queue each afternoon for one of his messages, then formulated a response, part intelligent debate and part creative play, with quirky humor or irony to lift his spirits. We mused on existentialism, how language shapes thought, poetry versus songwriting, whether pain is more physical or mental, and Doris Day. I felt a sense of meaning, believing I was being at least a little helpful to another human. Though we never saw each other, he once wrote that I made him feel "seen." After he died, his wife said something similar. It was humbling.

We all want to feel "seen," don't we? *Seen* is the sense that someone else acknowledges who you are, glimpsing the invisible thread that you are following, that is your one-and-only life. In fact, I felt *seen*, too. Relationships that are mutually supportive can be their own form of Joy Habit.

Crafting replies called on my love affair with words and ideas, challenging myself with each poke of the Send button. That he was in the process of dying the whole time stirred up sadness in me, but also gratitude. Those funny, thought-provoking emails were a gift. Yes, it was joy that lingered during those too-fast months.

Do you have a Joy Habit?

Each of us is unique in what cultivates joy in our lives. At some point, most of us have practiced a Joy Habit, whether it's as simple as a morning run or nurturing a batch of sourdough starter each night to keep it alive.

174

Over time your Joy Habit may evolve. You might have grown up playing piano, jamming on all those keys, only to decide at 37 that the guitar is what really rocks your soul. Maybe you have a Joy Habit that you lost and found. Remember Etta who lost one of her sons and started running in her late 50s? Thanks to a letter from a faraway girl, she rediscovered her Joy Habit of running, and her feet propelled her through grief.

With the death of someone you love, with the disruption of your daily rituals, habits, and routines, sometimes your Joy Habit dies, too. That's when the emotional inertia can settle in. For me, writing each morning has been my most life-affirming Joy Habit for decades—it's just who I am. Yet, after the death of my mother and Ruth, I stopped writing for almost three years. How could I write when death seemed to be stalking people I loved and ultimately me? It seemed pointless, on par with navel-gazing. I had no energy, passion, or self-belief to open a notebook and scrawl even one word.

What I discovered, though, as I implemented my Tiny-Come-Back-to-Your-Senses Ritual, first before bedtime and then again in the morning, is that the ritual created both a break in the grief and an opening to go farther. Standing on my deck, mindfully focusing my five senses, experiencing as fully as possible whatever was happening in my immediate world, reminded me I'm alive.

That set of sensory rituals was just the force I needed to impact my emotional inertia. After so long being in my dark little bear cave, being a thing at rest staying at rest, I was moving toward action, poking my head out of the cave. I was becoming a person in motion who wanted to stay in motion a little longer each day.

One morning, after practicing my good-morning-to-the-morning ritual, I came back in the house, made a cup of tea, and went to my study. I moved piles of books and papers off of my desk and grabbed the first notebook that turned up. I blew dust from my dragonfly lamp, rummaged in a drawer for an old-fashioned yellow school pencil, and started writing about all that my senses brought to my awareness that morning.

I wrote about the alternating rushing and trickling of water moving through river stones and the way it could sound like distant voices, a conversation I could hear but not understand. I jotted down how I heard an osprey, but couldn't find her with my binoculars. I described the mist drifting in the shallow canyon above the water, as if the river was being reincarnated as air. I noted one fir dripping dew into mud, as kind of impatient finger tapping, tapping, tapping.

Many times since, I've looked back at my scribbled phrases. I read that my misty hair was cold as it clung to my cheek that morning. As I stepped back into the house, my toes were numb, and my cats, Muir and Maya, sniffed them excitedly as if I'd brought them back "a really good river story told through scents."

Then there's this pair of lines: "The world has always had a language before words. It speaks to you through your senses." That's how my tiny rituals got their name.

I moved through the rest of that long-ago day with a little more energy and ease. It felt so good to write again, to hold the pencil, to hear the lead scraping paper forming words, and to see my own craggy handwriting on the white, faintly lined page. Writing is my endorphin-maker. The next morning, *Gimme more endorphins please!* So after waking and doing my tiny sensory ritual, I was back at my desk.

After that, I might miss a morning or two of writing to sleep, to an early meeting, or to linger by the river, though mostly I was writing every morning. My Joy Habit was reestablishing itself. I was moving out of persistent grief and spending more time in joy, that feeling of well-being and belonging to the world again.

Lifting myself out of the deepest grief I've ever experienced, I wrote a line that continues to carry me forward. "Can't waste all this aliveness on sadness. Must be. Must do. Must make some corner of the world better." Of course, you can't make any corner of the world better until you get your own little corner back up and running.

Not long after my writing habit took hold, I was able to build in another Joy Habit that hadn't completely left me in my loss but had become erratic—my morning walk. So, the healing process looked like this: first I started my Tiny-Come-Back-to-Your-Senses Ritual, then I added on my Joy Habit of writing, and then my Joy Habit of walking piggybacked on those actions. I can't convey, really I can't, how my tiny rituals and Joy Habits brought me back to life.

What's your thing?

Writing, walking, singing, or for that matter, coaching sled dogs to lunge through snow or knitting sweaters for penguins (other Joy Habits I've discovered in my universe), may not be your "thing." What is your "thing," that activity that draws you in and fuels your joy?

Review:
Stepping Stones to Help You in Your Loss Journey

 You are meant to live with joy and your body knows it. Sometimes your mind generates attitudes about grieving that complicate your healing, while your body can help reconnect you to joy and well-being.

 Suffering can become a corrosive habit without Joy Habits to counterbalance it. The longer you stay in suffering, the harder it will be to know joy again, because your animal brain likes what's known and familiar, even if the known and familiar is suffering.

 Habits are more than just behaviors or a mindset. While destructive habits can erode your physical and mental health, habits that cultivate joy can improve your immune system and support healing on multiple levels. Healing is rooted in the concept of wholeness. Joy Habits strengthen your resilience and reduce the time you spend in pain.

 Laughing and singing, along with other joy-cultivating habits, trigger the release of endorphins, the body's natural pain relievers and pleasure enhancers.

 The formula for a Joy Habit is: **Actively Doing** + **Regularly Doing** + **Cultivating Joy** = **Well-being**.

 You begin a Joy Habit with intention, and with consistent practice, it becomes automatic.

Joy Habits move your life forward. Whether your grief takes the shape of inactivity or hyperactivity, Joy Habits are an important force for interceding in your emotional inertia.

13

Minding

Practice the art of paying attention

First there were shells, then wings, then pretty petals. If you place each one in your palm, you're holding a half-billion years of hard work. Time evolves. Pay attention. This moment is so brief.

— from my notebooks, December 2020

A few years ago, I had a strange dream and wonderful vision. In it, we were all ravens. Have you ever seen the way a raven walks? They have a lurching, rocking gait. I was on Clam Beach, a few miles from home, and we were all ravens strutting and swaying about, dragging our tails in the sand, leaving a trail of z's as the feathers brushed back and forth with each step.

As raven people, we were just looking around and listening. I felt this communal curiosity. Mostly none of us were talking, though there were a few random squawks as one of us let the rest of us know about some discovery. I understood that we wanted to be quiet so we could hear the ocean and all the subtle sounds around us. The waves crashing and retreating reminded me of thousands of wings flapping at once, a kind of birdy applause. I realized the earth itself had a sort of music, a mix of scraping and sizzling and unseen voices below the surface humming.

Because we were ravens, with our eyes situated on the sides of our heads, we would each take a few swaggering steps, then tilt our heads to the left and look down at something on the beach to see what it was. Maybe there'd be a knot of wet seaweed or eel grass washed up, a halo of insects buzzing and hovering around it. Or there'd be a soggy sneaker or a gelatinous jelly fish or a piece of driftwood crusted with barnacles. I could see pearl-sized pools of water in some barnacles.

As the left eye explored whatever was on the ground, the right eye was aimed at the clouds and bits of sun coming through openings. Light seeped down on all of us, making our black raven feathers shimmer slightly purple. We were lovely shiny beings, perfectly content to be wandering around Clam Beach, listening and looking.

I was one raven at the edge of the surf, enchanted to peer down and find I had raven feet that couldn't feel the Pacific's usual coldness. I was part of the all that was going on, but also separate, a witness, watching. Then I noticed all the ravens had something under their right wing. I cocked my raven head back and forth trying to figure out what was under those wings. Soon I realized I had something pressed to my ribs, under my right wing.

Out of the blue, I said, "We all have a box of luminous things." I was startled to hear my human voice come out of my raven beak, saying those exact words. I woke up immediately, my eyes opening into the shadowy ceiling of the bedroom, moonlight in dusty rays coming in through the window.

But the story doesn't end there. I felt compelled to get up and go to the window. I don't know why. I just had to go to the window. At that time there was a huge huckleberry bush outside the bedroom that my husband had thinned and shaped to be more of a bushy tree, open limbs below with a lush crown of small, oval leaves. As I looked out, I thought my husband had somehow surprised me by weaving white Christmas lights into all those leaves. The huckleberry was bright with hundreds of little white twinkling lights.

Dazzled and happy, I just stood there, gazing. Finally, it dawned on me. They were not white lights, but hundreds of beads of dew hanging from the leaves and branches, and the moonlight was coming through each of them at just the right angle to create true brilliance. As I took it all in, energized, feeling my heart beating like a dancing raccoon in my chest, the huckleberry began to dim and quickly go dark. It returned to its regular, predawn bush-ness.

I'd seen how the ordinary can be extraordinary, if I pay attention and be mindful of whatever is happening around me. Wonder and curiosity are underappreciated paths to well-being.

The experience felt timeless, but it was likely less than a couple of minutes. It was a little after 4 a.m., February 11, 2017. I know because when I rose later, I wrote it all down, a mess of lead because I can't write as fast as I can remember. I had to capture the dream and the vision, tuck them into the pages of my notebook the way I used to press rosy, autumn maple leaves into my journal to hold on to them. What makes writing like magic is it helps relive an experience in the process. Later on, reading my scribbles and deciphering my words, the experience can be recreated again and again in my mind.

Just writing all of this pulls me back into that odd dream and exhilarating sight, making me ask again, *Where did it all come from?*

The mind is bigger than the brain.

The mind is an amazing place. But what is it? The mind. There are many theories, but no one really knows. What's agreed is that the mind makes itself known through thoughts, ideas, language, imagination, memories, dreams, judgements, beliefs, moods, decision-making, logic, creativity, planning, an array of emotions, and consciousness.

Most importantly the mind is self-awareness. My mind is my "I" and "me," just as your mind is your "I" and "me." Regardless of whatever else your body is up to, without a mind, you're not alive in any meaningfully human way.

The mind is usually described as rising from and being a function of the brain, which is physical and visible, that is, if you could peek inside your skull. The mind, however, is something different, transcendent and invisible.

The brain is a spongey, wet, maze-like mass, resembling a giant walnut, lumpy, coiled, and with two halves. It roughly adds about three pounds to your scale, literally, it's mostly fat, the fattiest organ in the body. It comprises about 86 billion interconnected neurons, that is, nerve cells, that are credited with making thought, consciousness, and all that we consider to be "the mind" possible. Through chemical and electrical processes, a group of neurons generates waves of energy that pour out to neighboring groups of neurons and from those, spreads to more neurons, and you have the beginning of a thought. It all happens in tiny fractions of a second.

Your mind is energy.

As sensory data coming in through our various senses reaches the brain—data from the environment immediately surrounding you as well as from within you—the brain's neurons react. At any time, the brain is processing a chaotic storm of input, allowing you to read this page while making sure you still have a pulse and can sit upright in your chair.

Out of this constant, diverse, brain energy, the mind spontaneously emerges. This is where science and magic seem to merge. We go from a physical tangle of neurons spreading waves of energy, to, poof, the invisible mind doing all of its busy mind stuff.

Your brain and your mind are always engaged in a little metaphysical dance—part physics, part beyond physics—your animal body showing off its miraculous human mind.

New research suggests the mind may not only live in your brain, but elsewhere in your body, especially in your heart and intestines. These organs also have networks of neurons. So, it's true—you can know something in your heart and that gut feeling may actually be an opinion.

Some studies suggest the mind exists at the level of each of your cells, after all, cells live on energy. The mind may even extend beyond the body, your mind leaking its energy into my mind.

Who hasn't looked at someone they love and felt a little electricity, that glance sparking an instant connection, one mind knowing what another is thinking? There's also a theory called quantum mind or quantum consciousness, linking quantum physics, how the universe works, and the idea that there is one cosmic mind or intelligence that we're all part of. The mind remains among the greatest mysteries for both philosophical inquiry and scientific research, both of which are only possible because of . . . the mind.

What's important to understand here are three ideas. First, as we've been discussing, your mind is energy entangled with your brain, body, and senses, and they're always interacting with each other. You can't affect one without affecting the others. Second, your mind is you, that self-aware "I" and "me." Third, your mind is relational. In order for there to be an "I" and a "me," there has to be some concept of "not me" or "other."

We always exist in relationship to others, whether that's living beings, such as humans, ravens, or glowing shrubs, or nonliving things, such window glass, dew drops, and moonlight. Remember the baby brain? Early in our development as tiny humans in the womb, our first sense is touch as our developing body distinguishes self from the rest of its placental universe.

This relational aspect of your mind is one reason why loss is so disorienting. Your mind is constantly generating the concept of who you are, and it always involves others, our lives a web of relationships. Remove someone you love, someone who's an essential ingredient in that concept of you but is now missing, and your mind develops a kind of limp. By the way, this same mind-wounding process happens with other types of losses, too, such as those triggered by a pandemic or a war, where key, life-affirming rituals, habits, and routines are broken or removed entirely. Your mind is resilient, and eventually it will devise a new concept of you, one way or another.

The question is, in the aftermath of loss, will you actively focus your mind to help it design a new you that aligns with the person you want to become? Or will you let your mind fabricate a new you out of that chaotic onslaught of input? You'll still be *you*, but it could be a persistently suffering you rather than a *you* cultivating joy in your life every day.

There's the mind, then there's being mindful.

"Pay attention. Be mindful of what you're doing." I can still hear my mother's voice saying that throughout my childhood. The words were offered as a caution, say, to not knock over a glass of milk reaching across the table for a barbecued chicken leg, or to not cut off a fingertip being too fast and clumsy with the scissors.

Did you hear those words as a kid? Actually, pay attention and be mindful is really good advice for life in general.

While my mother tended to say those words in a negative context, to ensure I avoided some minor disaster, the advice works best when viewed as a prescription. Forget "take two aspirins and call me in the morning." Instead, pay attention and be mindful so you can actually experience the morning.

Because so much is going on in our brains and our minds perpetually, hours, days, years, and decades can pass with only a vague idea of how we got from point A to point B. It's disconcerting enough when our minds are so distracted that we don't know how we got from our garage to the grocery store. Worse is suddenly wondering one afternoon how we got from 2001 to 2021? Yikes, what happened to all that time and a big chunk of life?

It's easy for a mind pulled in many directions to feel unanchored in any one moment. In the era of social media and devices in every pocket or purse, the brain is overloaded with input, the mind bombarded with images and information more than ever.

Can you remember what you were doing on this date and at this time a year ago, what about two years ago or seven years ago? Unless something wonderful or awful happened at those points, you probably can't summon a very detailed memory of most moments of your life. A busy mind that doesn't pause a little each day to focus on *being* in that day can leave you feeling as if your life is just passing by, or maybe rushing away.

Ever feel like your one-and-only life is little more than a leaf floating on a swift river?

Paying attention and being mindful can't stop the forward flow of time, but it can help you warp it a bit in your favor. You can slow down time when you're numbly racing through your days. You can also speed up time when you're languishing in grief, despair, or anxiety.

If you've created a Tiny-Come-Back-to-Your-Senses Ritual and have been practicing it, you may have already experienced a little time warping. Standing on my deck, saying good morning to the morning, using all of my senses to take in whatever is happening around me, helps me slow down time. I'm trying to *be* in those few minutes. In the process, each minute seems to deepen and expand, so time assumes a more relaxed pace.

Joy Habits often have the opposite or a paradoxical effect on your sense of time, akin to being a time traveler. Where my tiny rituals stretch time, my Joy Habits seem to accelerate time, but in a good way.

For instance, when I'm mentally absorbed in writing, playing around with words and ideas, it can feel like I've stepped out of time completely. When I stop, I'll think I've only been writing a short time when in fact a few or several hours have passed. That's why, if I'm writing on a workday, I set a minimally obnoxious alarm to stop. When I'm mindfully engaged in my writing, though the time flies fast, I experience time deeply, slowly, almost as if it didn't exist at all. Odd? Yes, wonderfully odd. My Joy Habit and the time warp it creates leave me feeling more whole and better able to handle whatever else the day holds for me.

The reason tiny sensory rituals and Joy Habits are so effective in stimulating well-being is they intentionally focus our minds. My Joy Habits, like writing and walking, are forms of mindful meditation for me. I hesitate to even use the words *mindful* or *meditation* because they stir up different assumptions in different people.

Many believe meditation is about emptying the mind. While that's *not* the goal I'm suggesting to you, I have experienced an "empty mind," where there are no thoughts. It's a more-than-peaceful way of being. Unfortunately, it only lasted a few moments—seriously, seconds at most. Each time, I'd hear a voice in my mind, *Hey, I'm not thinking*, followed by, *rats, that was a thought and so is this.* The empty mind is quickly occupied.

One of the principles of nature is that it abhors a vacuum. Even outer space with all that blackness between stars that seems the epitome of emptiness, isn't empty at all, comprising a mysterious element called dark matter or dark energy. The human mind is similar, a vast inner space, and apparently it abhors a vacuum, too.

In short, the human mind is something of a thought junkie.

Being mindful is asking your mind to pay attention to something specific rather than helplessly letting itself be bombarded by every thought or bit of sensory data arising. Let me share a couple of analogies to help you get the gist of what I mean.

Have you ever been to a restaurant? Hmmmm, I'm writing that question right now in the middle of a pandemic. It's been nearly a year since I've seen the inside of a restaurant with friends, so I'm feeling a bit of loss asking the question.

I want you to think about the last time you met a friend or sweetheart for dinner at a bustling restaurant. Now, assuming your dinner companion's voice is audible and not drowned out by other sounds, you are listening intently to that one voice while other voices bubble all around you. That's what being mindful is like. Also, when the server brings your salad with arcs of red onions or your grilled salmon or that wedge of German-chocolate cake, imagine slipping a forkful into your mouth. Whatever it is, it smells marvelous, your mouth is doing a happy dance savoring it, and your mind is paying attention to all of that gustatory adventure, despite the fact that there are lots of other scents, dozens of voices in conversation, knives clinking plates, cars passing outside the window, the heating system is rattling, and one of the servers just dropped a plate of spaghetti and let out a groan.

Now for contrast, your companion just left the table for a moment, dinner is done, and you're sitting there not paying attention to anything in particular. You're just experiencing flow and chaos of the restaurant environment. What do you hear? You hear an enormous buzzing. Do you hear any one thing? No, just an amorphous, loud, aimless, hissing hum. That's how our mind can feel when it's not in mindful mode, especially during deep grief. Even feeling numb is typically characterized by a mind so overwhelmed with thought and emotion that it seems to freeze and hunker down in the grating buzz.

Ironically, if you consciously focus on the totality or oneness of the restaurant's buzzing, you can create a mindful experience out of it. I know, because I've done it. It's fun to feel like a bee in a giant hive—part of it and also separate from it at the same time. I've discovered I can feel it all as a vibration in my chest, as if the world around me is using my body to chant. Pretty cool, really, and powerful.

The mind can focus like a camera, from portrait to landscape. The key word is *focus*, as in, pay attention and be mindful.

In introducing your Tiny-Come-Back-to-Your-Senses Ritual, you are focusing your mind initially on just one of your five senses and paying attention to whatever sensory experience it brings you. In introducing and developing a Joy Habit, you'll be intentionally aiming your mind. You'll focus on doing one activity and mindfully experiencing it, initially for just minutes.

Brainy birds can teach us.

Maybe I dreamed of ravens because I'm a Corvid-lover. Corvid, in the bird-watching world, is the name of the family of birds that includes ravens, crows, blue jays, and magpies. They're often described as brainy birds, because they're good problem-solvers who can use tools, gesture with their beaks and feet, share a complex bird language and create new calls, hold deep memories, and know when they're being watched.

Ravens can even recognize individual human faces, my husband's face from mine or yours. Can you do that? Can you look at the faces of ravens and know who's who? Despite their bird-sized skulls, their brains are dense, comprising as many neurons as many mammals and some primates.

It's not their brain I love, however, it's their mind. If you think it's strange we don't know exactly what the human mind is, the mind of a raven is even more mysterious. The mind of a raven reflects imagination, emotions, empathy, planning, and play. Less social than crows, ravens typically mate for life and hang out in pairs. I've watch two ravens play with a chicken bone, one flying up and dropping the bone while the other swerved down to grab it in its beak, then fly up to drop it for the other to catch. I'm sure there's some scientific reason for that behavior. I say it was a raven relationship and they were busy making joy together.

Ravens are mindful. I think they strutted into my dream because I needed a mentor. Ravens have no problem sifting through all the sensory activity around them to focus on what matters most. That's the benefit of being an animal whose very survival depends on paying attention.

Did I mention we are animals?

Not long after my raven dream, I was out on Clam Beach in thin fog for a chilly walk. After a while, I realized a raven was ambling along parallel to me. I walked barefoot at the edge of the frigid Pacific, while Raven, with his rocking bird hips and three-toed footprints, kept up the pace along the wrack line, that place were bits of seaweed, driftwood, remnants of crabs, and other sea debris wash up on shore. When I stopped to pick up pretty stones, he stopped, seeming to watch me. When I angled up shore to check out a dead gull, he angled up shore, too, keeping the same distance between us. Then as I drifted back toward the surf, he ambled over to the dead gull. Raven poked it with his beak, then with a hop and fluttery leap he caught up to me.

"Are you waiting for a food treat?" I asked him or her. No answer. I pulled my pockets inside out, showing I had nothing to offer. We continued our hike together for more than a mile before another raven flew to a log up shore and squawked. Raven lifted up, twiggy legs kicking, into the air. He circled over me and flew toward the other raven, his companion, I assumed. "Namaste," I whispered, which I translate as the spirit in me honors the spirit in you.

I wondered why Raven had come along with me. Then my dream flashed through my mind, along with a Taoist parable about dreaming vs. reality. I thought, *What if instead of being a human who dreamed she was a raven, I'm really a raven dreaming she's a human?*

Review:
Stepping Stones to Help You in Your Loss Journey

 Paying attention and being mindful to what is happening around you allows you to see how the ordinary can be extraordinary. Wonder and curiosity are paths to well-being.

 Your mind is your self-awareness—it's your "I" and "me." Regardless of whatever else your body is up to, without a mind, you're not alive in any meaningfully human way.

 You brain is largely the physical source of your mind, though your gut, heart, and other parts of your body, possibly down to your cells, also contribute to what you think of as your mind. Your mind is energy entangled with your brain, body, and senses, and they're always interacting with each other. You can't affect one without affecting the others.

 Your mind is relational. In order for there to be an "I" and a "me," there has to be some concept of "not me" or "other." This relational aspect of your mind is one reason that the loss of someone you love can alter your sense of self.

 The degree to which you are paying attention to what you're doing and being mindful of what's happening in any moment affects your sense of time. When you're not paying attention or being mindful, it can seem like years pass in the blink of an eye or that your life is rushing past without you.

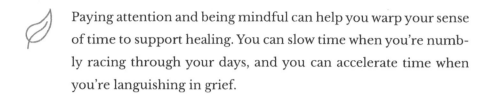 Paying attention and being mindful can help you warp your sense of time to support healing. You can slow time when you're numbly racing through your days, and you can accelerate time when you're languishing in grief.

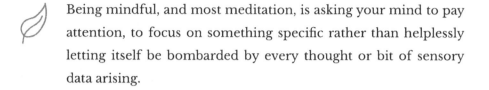 Being mindful, and most meditation, is asking your mind to pay attention, to focus on something specific rather than helplessly letting itself be bombarded by every thought or bit of sensory data arising.

 The mind, being energy and being powerful, connects us to other humans and animals in ways we can never fully understand.

14

Practice

Establishing a Joy Habit

Let's practice joy making.

What used to bring you joy? What might bring you joy that you've never tried before?

Even if you are at a place where you can't see joy emerging in your life, I want you to think about these two questions. I want to encourage you to create a Joy Habit, starting small, that you will initially piggyback onto your Tiny-Come-Back-to-Your-Senses Ritual. Over time, you will grow the habit, and ideally it will be an option for mending the broken places in your day that you've already identified.

Your Tiny-Come-Back-to-Your-Senses Ritual is about being fully present and deeply experiencing a few (or many) minutes of your day, enabling you to take a break from grief. Joy Habits are about action, *doing*, getting your mind, body, emotions, and/or spirit moving to cultivate joy into your life and carry you in the direction of your Feeling Intention.

Carefully chosen, consistent action exercises your resiliency muscle and spurs transformation. Such action helps you adapt to change, including the uninvited realities that go with the death of a loved one. Additionally, the right kind of repeated actions support your becoming process, your evolution toward a new you full of possibilities. If you're in the hibernating-in-a-bear-cave mode of grieving, then we want to draw you out into the sunlight for awhile. If instead you're pushing through grief with the blurred wings of a hummingbird perpetually busy, then we want to pause your flight so you can pay attention to the flower in front of you. It's about being intentional in our doing until it becomes a more automated habit.

Remember the formula for a Joy Habit? **Actively Doing + Regularly Doing + Cultivating Joy = Well-being.**

The Stanford School of Medicine's Well for Life initiative defines 10 life domains that contribute to your sense of wellness: stress and resilience, emotional health, physical health, meaning and purpose, sense of self, finances, spirituality or religiosity, social connectedness, lifestyle behaviors, and exploration and creativity. You don't need and won't usually achieve wellness in all domains. One person may live with an autoimmune condition that won't allow consistent wellness in the physical health domain, but may enjoy abundant wellness in the domains of social connectedness, spirituality, and creativity. Another person may struggle with social connectedness, but thrive in their sense of purpose, financial security, and living a healthy lifestyle.

What areas of wellness are most important to you? Your Feeling Intention is a clue.

Joy Habits will usually function in several domains. For instance, my Joy Habit of walking nurtures wellness in the domains of resilience, emotional health, physical health, spirituality, and exploration. Since my predominant Feeling Intention is to feel peaceful, walking feeds that intention.

If you are already engaging in a Joy Habit, then you can build on that habit and use it as a bridge through gaps in your day that aren't working well because of your loss. Otherwise, you have at least the two options I posed above: reigniting an old Joy Habit or initiating an entirely new one. You can be like Etta and start running again after decades, or like my Alaskan donor who quit kayaking after her husband died and later took up horseback riding.

Here's how to start a Joy Habit.

While moving your body tends to activate you in the mental, emotional, and spiritual realms as well as the physical, your options are not narrowed to running or horseback riding. My Joy Habits, besides walking, include writing, yoga and breathwork, sea kayaking, and cat juggling. Okay, my cat's decline being juggled, but the point is, your Joy Habit may be unusual and unique to you. For what it's worth, though, playing with my cats each evening is a Joy Habit for me and I'm pretty sure for them, too.

Then there are our neurochemical friends—endorphins! You'll recall that endorphins are the body's natural pain relievers and pleasure enhancers. While initially you'll start slow with your Joy Habit, the goal is to expand the time you spend involved in your Joy Habit to 30 to 60 minutes, or more, most days. You'll feel benefits from even a few minutes of doing something that taps your personal passions. Then, when that joy activity is performed for an extended time, your clever animal body will release endorphins and you'll experience that sense of flow, of time warping because you're so absorbed in what you're doing.

Let me share again the range of Joy Habits I've discovered in my work with people from all walks of life: Beekeeping, hiking, podcasting, biking, shooting hoops, kombucha making, photography, dog training, sculpting, meditation, weightlifting, rock hunting, running, quilting, fly tying, painting, composting, yoga, vegetable gardening, bench building, putting, coloring, stargazing, guitar playing, swimming, songwriting, dancing, slacklining, collecting driftwood, bread baking, tutoring, letter-writing to prisoners, recycling, hair braiding, goat raising, programming robots, online selling, cheesemaking, genealogy, jewelry design, video creation, journaling, woodcarving, and there's more!

Here are eight keys to a viable Joy Habit:

- **Active Not Passive:** Whatever you choose to do, it needs to activate you on some level. You want to be physically, emotionally, mentally, or spiritually doing something, or it's a temporary feel-good, distraction-from-loss behavior that provides momentary relief, though won't have an enduring impact on your joy or well-being. Meditation may seem passive, but in fact you are actively focusing on your breath, a mantra, or observing your monkey mind of random thoughts. So, in developing a Joy Habit, ask, how am I being active?

- **Consistently Doable:** If you're at a loss for where to start, consider what you might be able to do on a consistent basis, that is, every day or nearly every day, that could potentially carry you toward your Feeling Intention and joy. You need to like what you do. You may love running, the wind in your hair, the way each foot connects with the earth, and seeing what's happening in the corner of the world you are running through—great! While running may be good for you, if you hate running, your knees creak, and the neighbor's dog lunges at you every time, well, pick something else. Initially doing anything may require some push and pull to get past the emotional inertia, that's why you start small. Once you begin, it will typically be easy to keep going for awhile if you like what you're doing.

- **Promise of Well-Being**: Look at the list of 10 wellness domains and pick one or a few (not a bunch) where you'd like to grow greater wellness. Be expansive in thinking about how your Joy Habit could really be transformative, even if it seems humble at the outset. How can joy and/or your Feeling Intention be realized in doing it? Decide in advance how you'll know if your well-being is blossoming in a specific domain. Note at the outset what you are experiencing in a given wellness domain. Then after practicing your habit, especially after a week, a month, and several months, ask yourself if your well-being has shifted from that initial assessment.

- **Scalable**: Initially, choose an activity or focus that can be done for a few minutes as well as for an hour or more. Pick a habit you can scale up or down. You don't have to garden or shoot hoops or meditate for an extended period for it to be beneficial, especially early on when consistency trumps duration. While you may like the idea of tearing out a flower bed and putting in a winter vegetable garden—a big project—if you don't have the emotional or physical stamina for that, let alone the time, your gardening habit will likely not sprout. Instead, keep the grand vision but also break it down into the tiniest crumbs of doing. For instance, you could pull a few weeds, open a catalogue and pick three root vegetables you'll grow, sketch one concept for a raised planter box, or even scoop up a palm of soil, seeing what's in it, feeling it in your hands, sniffing it, and imagining what you could grow in it. The idea is to do your gardening, or whatever your habit is, in some form or other each day.

- **Variable:** Ideally, choose an activity that you can ultimately do at different times and places. Beekeeping could be a challenge, while meditation not so much. Still, think it's impossible to do your Joy Habit anytime-anywhere? Let me challenge your thinking, because if your habit can cultivate joy for you, then you really want to do it daily. One acquaintance who'd decided to take up vegetable gardening lived in a city center and travelled regularly for work. She surprised me with her ability to garden wherever she was. On one business trip, she left time between two meetings so she could visit a certain sidewalk vegetable stand, where she spent 15 minutes talking to the organic produce buyer about carrots. Another time, she brought a packet of lettuce seeds to give to her client, an elementary school teacher, to involve her students in food growing. She later visited the school and talked to the kids about their crops. She was thinking about gardening each day when she wasn't doing it, and thinking is a form of doing, as is engaging with others who share or could benefit from your passion.

- **Rainy-Day Strategy:** You are human and stuff happens. There will be days when your schedule is out of whack, your emotional inertia is fierce, or you're in one of your grief holes seemingly without a rope to climb out. In a moment when you're functioning well, decide how you'll coax yourself to action and carve out a sliver of time to do your activity even when you think you can't. The variable aspect is critical here. Have three- or five-minute options you can do right before bed as your last opportunity to *do* something. Okay, you may not want to take a run at midnight, that might make sleep harder when sleep is what you desperately need at the end of a rogue day. Instead, could you spend a few minutes thinking about a new running route to try the next day? What about practicing your pre-run stretches that won't over stimulate you? Or as an acquaintance did, could you lie in bed and mentally run for a few minutes before drifting off, imagining the rhythm of your legs on your favorite path, how your hips seem to lead you, your arms pumping back and forth, the sun heating your cheeks, or whatever comprises the experience of your Joy Habit?

- **Accountability:** Holding yourself "accountable" is actually a variation on your rainy-day strategy. Frankly, I find it a mixed bag as a resource for starting and sustaining your Joy Habit. You may want to have an accountability partner or small circle of friends you tell about your Joy Habit. Making your intentions a little public and/or having people you can call or text to coach you through the rough patches can help you stay on course. But. I need to offer one caution in the context of mourning and especially deep grief. For some, holding one's self accountable and sharing personal intentions with others don't lead to a supportive and nurturing environment—they generate significant stress on top of feeling overwhelmed. For some, loss triggers emotions related to failure, regret, remorse, and shame, so when they fall off course with their Joy Habit they can pummel themselves with negative self-talk, driving themselves deeper into despair. Choose accountability partners or circles carefully, ensuring they are loving, gentle voices of support that can only lift you up.

- **Keeping Momentum Visible:** Because tiny changes may initially look like modest results, it's good to have a visible reminder that you are making progress in actively and consistently doing your Joy Habit. The simplest way is to have a calendar pinned where you'll see it, a lot. Then each day, after you practice your Joy Habit, you cross off or draw a little smile or whatever on that day. As the week then first month passes, you'll have that visual proof that you are actually doing something to cultivate joy and well-being. There are other progress-tracking options, too, so be creative and be you. If journaling is your Joy Habit, your visual proof is all those hand-written pages adding up. If it's swimming, you might snap a selfie of your wet face (ideally smiling, but maybe grimacing if it was a tough swim) and upload each as a tile on your computer home screen. After awhile, your screen will fill with your face representing all those days you swam through. When I returned to walking after a hiatus, I'd bring back a twig, or when traveling in a city, a pebble or stray penny, and put it in a clear glass bowl. Within a month, I had three bowls, overflowing, and knew I'd come along way. Of course, by then I also felt healthier, more resilient, and was experiencing more joy in my days. Those sticks helped me stick to my habit-building until the well-being became more obvious.

Let's implement your Joy Habit.

There are a few ways to implement your Joy Habit depending upon where you are in your mourning process, the activity you've selected, and where the flow of your day is disrupted. Here I'm assuming that, for whatever reason, you're not regularly practicing a Joy Habit and could use a proven process to get started.

There are four basic steps, with a possible fifth:

- **Step 1: Extending Your Tiny Ritual:** After you have been practicing your three-minute Tiny-Come-Back-to-Your-Senses Ritual for some period (could be a little as a week or a few months), perhaps growing it to a five- or ten-minute practice, you add in your Joy Habit. Like your ritual, you start small. Typically, you'll start with 3, 5, 7, or 10 minutes engaging in your activity. While you can certainly keep going longer than that, it's best to start with a modest intention that you might exceed. It's okay to surprise yourself. If you set a larger intention, for instance 30 or 60 minutes, you leave yourself vulnerable to feeling failure if you fall short. Remember—consistency is essential. You will be practicing your Joy Habit every day, or nearly daily, and when you are still struggling with loss, your emotional inertia will be acute some days more than others.

- **Step 2: Practicing Daily:** There are a number of studies looking at how long it takes to create a habit, ranging from a couple weeks to several months. For now, aim for 30 days, a month, of doing your Joy Habit daily, though break that target down into seven-day intentions. Having some visual proof of your daily practice, as mentioned above, can be incredibly encouraging. It's harder to skip a day when you see all those reminders of how far you've come. How long it will take to turn your intentional activity into a true Joy Habit that you just do regularly without much thought is unique to you, the nature of your loss and grief, your level of wellness in the various life domains, the activity, and the mindset or level of intention you bring to this process.

- **Step 3: Growing Your Joy Habit:** During the first week, be gentle with yourself and focus on doing only three to ten minutes of your Joy Habit daily. There's no need to ramp up fast. It's not a race— it's an evolution. As you approach the 30-day mark and move beyond it (kudos to you!), you'll know when it feels right to extend the time spent doing your Joy Habit. In a perfect world, most aim for 30 to 60 minutes every day doing their Joy Habit. Of course, the perfect world doesn't exist, which is why if you can't get in 30 or 60 minutes some days, then do 15 or 7 or just 3 little minutes. Remember: It's scalable. Something is always better than nothing in generating well-being and avoiding the negative feelings that usually accompany a lapse. Your 30- to 60-minute practice may include starting with your Tiny-Come-Back-to-Your-Senses Ritual, or over time, you may detach your tiny ritual from your Joy Habit, practicing each at different times. The tiny ritual is intended to create a break from grief while opening space for growing a Joy Habit, though once a practice becomes a habit, you may not (always) need the trigger of your tiny ritual.

- **Step 4: Adapting Your Joy Habit:** Once your Joy Habit is, well, more habit-like, it's mobile. In other words, if you started your Joy Habit during your lunch break though find that the toughest point in your day is when you get home from work and feel an overwhelming longing for the one you love, then move your Joy Habit to the evening or repeat a version of it then. It's okay to allow yourself to experience and acknowledge that longing, though you don't want to spend every evening there. Once whatever grief emotion has blown into you, hold it for a few moments, be with it fully (short of self-harm, of course), tears or no tears, a yell or silently looking at the wall. Then move into your Tiny-Come-Back-to-Your-Senses Ritual, followed by practicing your Joy Habit for a bit.

- **Step 5 (optional): Establishing New Joy Habits:** As your becoming process unfolds through your tiny ritual and Joy Habit, you'll often be ready to take on more. Do it! There are also practical reasons to engage in multiple Joy Habits. For one, you're making more joy in your life and fulfilling your Feeling Intention. There's also the fact that some Joy Habits are easier to do at certain times and certain places than others. It takes more creativity to swim or sculpt in an airport, though meditation, sketching, or app designing are doable. Finally, aim for at least one Joy Habit that makes your body move, unless you have mobility or health challenges that prevent it. Physical movement is a powerful antidote to an overthinking mind.

In the early days, weeks, and months as you practice your tiny rituals and Joy Habits, revisit your Feeling Intention periodically. In the first 30 days, if you've placed sticky notes all over so you are constantly running into reminders of your Feeling Intention, use those notes both to reset your intention and to assess where you are with that feeling. At the end of each week and certainly the end of your first 30 days, pause and assess whether you're experiencing that feeling more often in your days and can see more joy, even if in small inklings. If the shift toward joy seems slight, it's still a shift. It's progress. Keep investing yourself each day in your tiny rituals and Joy Habits, knowing that transformation is happening. It's often not until we pause in our individual journeys to look back, to remember where we started relative to where we are now, that we realize we've already become new beings, more resilient and still evolving.

Section 4

Designing your Emotional Flak Jacket

15

Expecting

You can release your inner critic

Sometimes what you think is true is only a paper crane, the idea of a bird, not the real feathered being standing in a field cackling her song. Unfold your despair like origami, which is nothing more than creased paper and air. Make it into something else, your one-and-only-face, laughing.

— from my notebooks, April 2014

A muffled sighing or singing caught my attention. A whispering. It was in the pauses, when my husband stopped speaking to stave off a sob with a deep swallow. In that quiet, a high-pitched chattering emerged.

Rubbing a tear into his grey beard, my husband grappled with scraps of paper, the draft eulogy for his mother, Rose. I knew what he was thinking: Why this much emotion, this depth of loss? It was time, she was ready, we saw it coming, she was 94 . . . and a half, she would have added. Bits of time matter when you're very young or very old. Death is always a surprise and a dagger, even when anticipated. I stroked the hair at his temple and hugged his arm.

He began reading the eulogy again, practicing, feeling the pressure of performance expectations, until a swell of grief forced another pause. There, again, the high-pitched chattering. Our Muir cat, alive then and vibrantly alert, inched his way into the kitchen, stalking, and staring at a baseboard.

Even in the midst of grief, we couldn't ignore the curious call of something living in our kitchen. On hands and knees, we crawled along the baseboard, listening. Naturally, silence. We watched cat ears pivot and twitch, honing in on sound. Then, I heard it, a squeaking. Striped tail whipping, Muir pawed at a low drawer, and we pulled it out, sitting it on the floor. While the cat rattled through the serving dishes and pie tins looking for a good chase, we peered into the cabinet to find a deer mouse, surprised against the back wall, her soft white belly almost luminous, the liquid specks of her eyes shining out of the darkness.

Have you ever seen a deer mouse? They are adorable.

Coaxing her into a handkerchief, my husband whispered, "Hello peromyscus," the Latin name for deer mouse. He saw the crease of worry across my brow, and nodded, heading for the door, her long tail dangling from his cupped hands. Into the brisk air, he released her to the dense undergrowth below a redwood.

Life demands our attention even in grief. We had to clean the drawer and its contents, then we returned to the eulogy, the scent of bleach lingering.

My husband began again, his voice deep and comforting, an occasional tremble when it was time to say "my mother."

On the counter, above the mouse drawer, a headline on the cover of *The Economist* announced, "Now we are seven billion." *Seven billion minus one*, I thought, focused on our loss. Against such a massive collection of people, each death could seem insignificant. But no. We're large in at least a few lives. For months after our Rosie died, I'd pick up the phone to call her, then remember, *She's gone*, setting the receiver down to stare out of a window.

That night in the kitchen, my husband kept practicing his tribute, trying to be stoic, imagining the gathering of people who had high expectations for Rose's son. Each time he practiced the eulogy, he'd get a little farther, but still not all the way to the end before he had to glance up from his handwriting, pause, and gulp hard. Then, surprise, I heard that high-pitched chattering again. Muir sat in front of the drawer, green eyes pleading up at us, and moaned.

Frustrated as well as relieved, my husband set the eulogy on the counter and pulled out the drawer again. No one there. Crouching, I noticed a faint trail of iridescence inside the cabinet, a residue—the subtle oils of the mouse's fur—leading to an upper drawer. We slowly opened it, stuffed with summer tablecloths, holiday napkins, and dish towels. Suddenly we both heard a more urgent squealing that sent Muir leaping, tongue rattling, onto my husband's back, ready to lunge.

As we pulled back a towel, a basket of grey fur came to life, whiskered noses probing into the fresh air, black-pearl eyes catching their first glimpses of human faces. Ms. Mouse was a mother. We both felt a surge of joy, strange and welcomed. Life! Those tiny faces had us laughing and crying, hugging Muir cat snugly out of gratitude, and to keep him from pouncing on the moving mass of baby mice.

Each mouse was perhaps a half ounce or less. We both thought, *They want their mother.* "Well at least they have each other," I whispered as my husband, an only child, counted the siblings. If the swelling population of human beings makes us all more anonymous, then deer mice live in oblivion.

215

"Namaste," I said seven times, looking into each nearly identical simmering face, trying hard to see them as individuals. "Well, some hungry screech owl is going to get lucky tonight," my owl-man quipped to Muir, squirming in his arms. Grief at bay, my husband had shifted into to his owl biologist self. I frowned, then found a box to offer. Together we listened to 28 delicately clawed feet in confused motion, scrambling and scratching the cardboard. The room filled with their downy will to make sense of their suddenly changed circumstances. We could relate to that—the change, the missing mother.

Through the window, I watched my husband step into the night with his box of brand-new mice. Only a few stars were strong enough to pulse against the glare of a gibbous moon, partial but bright. Leaves and fern fronds shimmered, already dewy, when he bent and tilted the box into the understory. The seven soft forms slipped unseen into the shadows, quick as an exhalation.

I saw my husband speak something. Then he stood, looking into the sky for the several minutes, before coming back inside.

"Were you talking to the mice?" I asked. He smiled, "I just said, you're on your own, guys." We remained at the window, watching below the redwood for movement, but there was only a light breeze stirring leaves. "So what were you looking at?" I continued. Both of our cats crowded into the box at our feet, sniffing every corner, side and flap. "I was thinking about calling in an owl," he answered, "but decided not to."

Whose expectations are weighing you down?

It doesn't take being a wildlife biologist to understand how the balance of life must include death. An owl has to eat, too, right? What would happen to the burgeoning world of mice and humans if no one ever left? Still, recalling this memory now, I'm glad my husband didn't summon any owls for an easy meal that night. In the midst of loss, we needed new life. Who knows what happened to Ms. Mouse and her babies? They're certainly gone now.

We know we are all going to be taken by the hungry mouth of death eventually, but most of the time we want to stay with the ones we love in the world of "not yet." We're not ready to leave or to lose anyone we love, not yet.

We're also not ready to deal with all the expectations others place on us in the aftermath of a death, let alone the demands we heap on ourselves. There was no way my husband could deliver his eulogy tearless.

So what?

That phrase became a mantra for me through multiple losses. I've spoken it silently in my mind, whispered it under my breath, offered it as a calmly wise reply, and yes, more than a few times, stressed and hurt, I've spouted it like a cranky little kid, feeling only a little foolish and wonderfully liberated.

So what?

It's the best mantra I know for helping you deal with other people—and also with your sometimes judge-y mind. In fact, much of the time, if you pause and pay attention to the nagging judgements stomping around inside your head, you'll find they don't belong to other people. Those demands and disappointments belong to you—they are you assuming what others expect and speculating that they're finding fault with you.

Death is the ultimate reminder that judgement is a waste of time and emotion for both judge and especially the judged, you. Expectations, judgements, criticism, and other shackles of opinion don't outlive us. Someday there will be no one to remember whether you cried or didn't cry and whether that was right or wrong of you.

By the way, in terms of cry versus dry when we're grieving, as we've discussed, there is no right or wrong behavior. Some of us are criers—

hey, I represent that remark—and some of us are desert dry, no tears, yet have a lot going on inside that's unseen.

As it turned out, delivering his eulogy was not the biggest emotional hurdle for my husband in hosting a celebration of his mother's life. The grief stoker was the venue.

Rose didn't want a funeral—she wanted a party. She envisioned her close, extended family babbling and joking together at her favorite restaurant called Buck's, and my husband promised her that party. Unfortunately, when a person lives to be 94½, she runs the risk of outliving her favorite places. Not only was the owner gone, the restaurant had changed hands multiple times. Beyond worn, dirty, and dusty, nothing was set up for a party when we arrived, and some of the kitchen equipment didn't work. The nice young couple hired to do the catering borrowed a portable stove, but they didn't know much about cooking for a group. The anticipated Buck's savory meal was a bland, sorry display of food piled in mismatched bowls and warped silver trays balanced over flaming cans of Sterno.

In essence, Buck's no longer existed. My husband was an angry, self-reproaching, mother-grieving knot of worry who could only focus on how he'd let his mother down and disappointed the family.

You know what, though? No one came for the food. Everyone was there for Rose, and though my husband couldn't accept it at the time, they were there for him, to support and hug and cry and especially laugh with him. Ask anyone who was there, and they'd tell you how sweet it was to be together and to hear my husband's deep, if quivering, voice speak of love.

To this day, he feels he failed at his mother's going-away party. Self-blame is an insidious form of grief that holds you down like a boot to your chest. As a leader, I used to tell my team, do your best, just remember you can't do better than your best—trying to do that is a kind of insanity. Also, from day-to-day and moment-to-moment your best changes.

As human beings, we like to think we're in control, but in truth, we can only influence tiny nooks in our universe. When we're grieving, our best is not our best. At the same time, we are often our worst critics. Do your best, then let go of the rest. Let me also add an additional insight here. I'll be blunt.

Dead people don't care.

The people we've lost don't have expectations nor can they be let down. If your loved ones do exist in some heavenly or otherwise sentient form, they're now all-knowing. They see into your heart and recognize the good intentions dwelling there. They probably have a sense of humor, too. I've got to think Rosie was amused by it all, except for her son's angst.

As for your circle of living others, they'll understand, like our family did, that stuff happens. They won't mind the funky, stained table cloths or that the chicken was so tough it could be used as a weapon. If they do complain or give you a hard time, intentionally or unintentionally, remember this—So what? They'll get over it, so you get over it. Okay?

We all need an Emotional Flak Jacket.

So much is happening in the world as I write this book. A scary virus is stalking the globe, the U.S. is dealing with the most bizarre presidential election in memory, protective face masks are political, and buying a head of organic lettuce requires almost paranoid vigilance for the personal space around you. If you won't wear a mask against the virus, there's another reason to wear one. The West is becoming smoke and smudged earth—wildfires seemingly everywhere.

Loss is such a small word for how wounded the world feels now. At the same time, it's what's connecting us, too. We're all navigating it in our own way, yet together. I think back to a certain autumn day when I realized how literally we may be a part of each other.

Ash fell as white petals over everything that afternoon—caught in ferns and spider webs, drifting into my lap, clinging to my hair, and dusting shards of cheese, carrots, almonds, and kiwi-fruits. I ate from a plate decorated with a black bear who looked flecked with dandruff. Probably it wasn't a good idea to have lunch outside when the largest fire in California's history, an hour and a half south of me, had already burned more than 1 million acres.

I peered through hazy air for the sun. It was a salmon-colored tunnel, pretty but surreal, a bright portal in the grey roof that was the sky that day and for weeks beyond.

Suddenly, I couldn't help wondering what I was breathing in and whom I may be consuming. The flames had taken in homes and humans, forests and who knows what living within them. What and who was in that ash? Most people could flee, but not all. How do you tell a deer or raccoon to evacuate? How do you warn a banana slug to pack up and move on? A banana slug only has one foot and it's slow.

I've never taken communion in the church sense, but that day, I felt a communion with the forests, animals, and people caught by flames. I bit the almond and crunched the carrots. I blew away ash, but couldn't avoid it riding in on the air. I savored the square of cheddar that stuck briefly to the roof of my mouth, followed by the kiwi, juicy-tart on my tongue. When you receive the wafer and wine, what is it the pastor or priest says? Do this in remembrance?

We live in each other and through each other. That's not just poetic, it molecular. It's also at the core of remembering.

In recent years, loved ones have lost everything to fires that keep ravaging the West. My cousin by marriage woke in the middle of the night in October 2017 to a literal fire storm sweeping up her Santa Rosa street. Hot wind, thick with smoke, blew at 50 to 60 miles per hour, forcing her and her husband out of their home with little more than the clothes they were wearing. Her neighborhood was left a charred mess of homeless chimneys, melted metal, and sooty, grey powder everywhere.

Later, picking through the rubble, she found her parent's wedding rings. Gone for years, her parents had been married for 67 years, beloved elders of an extended family. Treasure took on a new meaning, found not on a sunken ship, but in two simple wedding bands tougher than a blaze.

When every material possession is taken away, what sustains us? It's the connections to the people we love, even if they exist only as memories.

Wedding bands. It wasn't the value of the gold, but the artifacts of a relationship, the love she witnessed between the two people who created her, adored her, and would comfort her if they could. They were there in those rings. She could hold two circles of gold, feeling their presence inside her.

Because my life has been so shaped by fire, I feel these losses viscerally. It's more than mind, emotions, and spirit processing them. When the stark, post-fire images and personal loss stories emerge, I feel them in my physical being.

For instance, I smell burnt hair. It's not something you intentionally want to remember, to re-experience. As a child, I didn't know what that odd scent was or what triggered it. I only knew it made me nauseated and anxious. It wasn't until my mother caught her hair on fire, smoking a cigarette while using hairspray, that I had a clue. There it was—that smell, as her strands became wicks. My father dowsed it, and she wasn't hurt. We all laughed. Processing this snippet of family history over time, I think the sensory memory of burnt hair lodged in me as a toddler in that burning room.

That slightly sulphury scent of singed hair rises sporadically inside me during fire season in the West. (Hmmm, when did I, we, start thinking of fire as a season?) I'd prefer to be ambushed by the earthy-spicy scent of rosemary, but sometimes you don't get what you want.

It's as if there is really only one fire that just repeats itself inside me. It's part of that Swiss Army Knife-like quality of loss. There's this one reality and it's multi-faceted. Fire resides in the tissues, the blood, all the organic machinery, and the 37 trillion cells that comprise this body of mine.

The body remembers.

Does it freak me out, the sudden smell of burning hair? Oddly, no—that is, not anymore. While I've not been able to block it, I've defused it. Over many years, my Emotional Flak Jacket, part of my life-support system for living with loss, has helped me reframe the experience.

What do I mean when I say Emotional Flak Jacket? It's a mindset version of an old idea for self-protection. Physical flak jackets were developed during World War II to shield pilots from flying fragments and debris projected by explosive weapons. Memories, whether purely mental or deeply sensory, can feel like shrapnel coming at us. Especially disturbing memories, where we relive elements of traumatic events and the deaths of people we love, can feel like explosions, fragments of experience piercing our well-being and destroying joy.

An Emotional Flak Jacket is a mental toolbox, a range of mindsets, you can assemble as you move through grief, mourning, and your process of becoming. It enables you to dodge or deflect grief boomerangs, those out-of-the-blue moments when you long for the one you loved and find yourself weepy or unexpectedly blue. Your Emotional Flak Jacket also helps you deal with new losses in the future, whether another death or the ordinary day-to-day challenges of living.

What do I do when the burnt hair wafts into my consciousness? If it's subtle, nothing other than acknowledge it and let it go. If it persists, I pull fresh rosemary from a shrub in my yard, rub it on my wrists, and breathe in the aroma. Alternatively, I dab lavender oil on my upper lip so that I drift to sleep in a bed of lavender rather than a scent tied to fire.

We'll explore other components of creating your Emotional Flak Jacket as we move through this section of the book. Just know that the mind is malleable, that is, shapeable and adaptable. You can aim its power to be a protector and a healer, to collaborate with you rather than clobber you.

While the wildfires surge on, the internal fire is actually one I can contain. Why? These increasingly deadly fire episodes remind me that I live, in part, for others.

Living for others is a way to hold on to your others.

Are you living for someone you've lost? I am. Many others are, too. Living for others, especially those who were young when they died, can be a motivation for moving forward with your life. Living for others is often a factor in answering the question, who do I want to become?

One of the people who helped me believe in the possibility of this book, because of his belief that everyone has a book in them, is a young guy named Chandler, still in his 20s at this point, whom I've never met, only encountered through his virtual talks. He built a wildly successful business in a handful of years essentially encouraging people to tell their stories. His goal is to help birth at least 100,000 books. He insists books change lives and each book can impact at least 10 people, so more than a million lives could be transformed if, and likely when, he succeeds. No small goal, but why?

A bracelet on Chandler's wrist says it all in an acronym, WWKD (What Would Kendall Do), and a phrase, Make Him Proud. Kendall was his close friend. At 20, hanging out with Chandler and other friends on the upper deck of a ship, Kendall was, in a random, awful instant, knocked over the rail by a piece of moving equipment, falling two stories to his death. While trying to process what happened to his friend, how he'd been standing just inches from him one minute and gone the next, Chandler learned his grandmother died. Talk about transformation.

Chandler's life changed in the days and weeks after these losses. He redefined who he wanted to become, including living for more than himself. Kendall died with a book draft, and Chandler published it. Since then, he and the idealistic team he's attracted is driving more than a book a day into print, written by people from almost every continent with a story to tell that might help someone else.

When I look at my long career in philanthropy, supporting and advising individuals and families in how they can create meaningful legacies through charitable giving, it's clear that helping others is a key element of an Emotional Flak Jacket. I'm blessed to be able to do such work, which feeds my well-being, but there's more to it.

Helping others is a powerful strategy for transforming your losses. Whether donating to a cause or volunteering in the community or reaching out to a troubled friend, do you feel better when you help others? Most do.

For instance, the families I worked with after the crash of Flight 800, mostly parents, knew they couldn't bring their child back. They could, however, help their daughter or son live on by helping some other daughter or son. Countless students are going to college or technical school thanks to scholarships created out of loss. Such gifts are a form of unconditional love—one grieving family touching the life of a young stranger with a dream.

To help others is to enable the one you love, their passions and their spirit, to live on. You know what I mean?

When you're feeling overwhelmed and bewildered, it's so normal to think, Why bother? It's understandable to get pulled back toward sadness and the limbo of loss. Sometimes you need to spend a little time there, because you will always miss your people and special animals. Also, the world can be mean at times. But. It helps no one, especially you, if you get stuck there.

When those moments emerge like a fog out of who-knows-where, I let myself grieve a little and remind myself—I can't waste this gift of life. My sisters didn't get to become all they deserved to be. To keep falling down a well of sorrow or numb despair is to pull them down, too. So, I think, *Let's go, let's keep going.* My self-talk is plural. I get to be here for me and for them, and every moment is full of possibility. That's not a sentimental idea, it's a truth.

There is one caveat to living for others: Don't burn out.

Several points in my life, feeling driven to do, do, do more, not wanting to waste the gift of life, I reached a point of burn out. Mentally and physically exhausted, I eventually ended up with autoimmune issues, because the immune system can be exhausted, too. It's only in recent years that I developed two mindset tools for achieving balance rather than burn out.

One I've already mentioned: the dead don't care. You and I are the only ones really judging how well we're using our gift of life, so maybe we need to rethink what it means to live well in every sense of the phrase. Living well is not only outwardly doing well and being there for everyone else, but also inwardly feeling well and being there for yourself.

The other mindset? If I'm not properly caring for me, I'm also neglecting them, the ones I live for.

Now, when I don't think I have time for a walk, a little kayaking, yoga, meditation, or whatever might provide a healthy break from too much striving, I do something nurturing for my *Others*. My *Others* are my sisters, my parents, and the many I've lost and live for. I suggest to myself, *If they were here, maybe they'd like to walk the beach looking for sand dollars or pause for a dance with one of my kittens to Pharrell Williams singing his* Happy *song.* Yes, I make assumptions about what my *Others* might enjoy, and they do like dancing with cats.

I call this mindset of living for others being an avatar. When you're an avatar, you are the embodiment of the ones you love. When you take care of yourself, you're loving them.

Do you ever move through your days using your eyes to see for your beloved Others? Using your body to experience something soothing or exhilarating for your beloved Others? Try it. Unless your grief is too raw that being an avatar for the one you love, even briefly, is too painful, try it.

Review:

Stepping Stones to Help You in Your Loss Journey

Life requires our attention despite our loss and grief. Tending to the day-to-day tasks can help you manage or even contain grief a bit while moving you forward in a balanced way. You may not be able to handle all the demands, though completing some is grounding when you may otherwise feel lost in loss.

Having a mindset of "So what?" is a surprisingly powerful way to avoid being pulled into a grief hole by unrealistic or unfair expectations. It helps to realize that you, too, are a source of expectations, and you can release them with "So What?".

While it may seem blunt to acknowledge: Dead people don't care. In other words, if you are trying to live up to perceived expectations from the person you've lost, stop. Your loved one doesn't have expectations nor can they be let down. If they exist in another realm, then they are all-loving and don't want you to suffer.

We live in each other and through each other. That's not just poetic, it molecular. It's also at the core of remembering. During good times and especially bad, what sustains you is the connections to the people you love.

An Emotional Flak Jacket is a mental toolbox, a collection of supportive mindsets that enables you to manage grief, deal with new losses in the future, and tackle the ordinary day-to-day challenges of living.

227

An avatar mindset is when you find meaning in your life in part by living for the person you've lost. It can be a helpful mindset for moving forward with your life and being compassionate with yourself, as long as it doesn't lead to feeling overwhelmed and burned out.

 Helping others through volunteerism, simple and regular acts of kindness, or philanthropic giving is another way to enable the one you love to live on, both in you and in the lives of other people.

16

Missing

Sometimes you let go, other times you let in

A friend, sightless since birth, said there are two kinds of blindness. "Either you see nothing, or you see everything, but the one you love." You think of that, looking at binoculars, camera, a pair of glasses on the desk that belonged to eyes now gone. What you long to see, can't be seen, so you hold on to those things, feeling your way forward.

— from my notebooks, January 2018

Sitting on the patio of one of my donors who funded programs for girls in India, I asked her why she decided to give. Nina, a mother of two adult daughters and a grandmother of three, listed several logical reasons related to her belief that those who are blessed with much should share with those less fortunate. We moved on to talk about whether investing in bikes for girls in rural India so they could safely attend school would be a good choice for her. Yes, a great idea. Then she said, "Do you really want to know why I give?"

Nina told me a story about washing baby clothes as a young mother. Her first and only child at the time, a girl, was barely a toddler when she died from a random fall. Then a year or so later, after deciding to "try again," Nina miscarried. Heartbroken twice, she kept accidentally opening the same drawer that held her little girl's baby clothes that she'd saved for her next baby. The sight of teeny leggings and doll-sized dresses dropped her to her knees in tears every time. Believing there would be no more babies, along with the specter of opening that drawer and being "stabbed with grief," as she put it, she decided to give the clothes away to another mother who needed them, perhaps barely getting by or fleeing an abusive boyfriend.

Before she could give the baby garments away, she had to wash them. Though already clean, she still felt compelled to wash every item. She shared an incredibly detailed memory of the process. There were soft pink and yellow socks light as autumn leaves and a white bunting with bear ears. "I called her my little cub," Nina remembered, smiling.

She painstakingly washed each piece by hand. As she dipped a baby shirt with a bunny or flower on it into soapy water, she unleashed a flood of memories with her little girl. Water poured through sleeves, and all she could focus on was the absence of arms. She pinned the clothes to dry on a line in sunlight, describing how they reminded her of little empty bodies blowing in the wind, as if "my sweet girl just flew away." Once dry, the small pile of baby clothes rested on her bed, and she kneeled in the sheets beside it. Holding each tee-shirt or tiny trouser to look at it one last time, she gave it a slow sniff as if trying to breathe into her body whatever might be lingering of her little girl. Then she folded it all into a box.

She explained how surreal and painful the process was—no wiggly struggle, no milky scent, no familiar hot-baby warmth to any of the clothes. They were just fabric and air. As awful as it was, Nina said that it wasn't until she'd done that odd, letting-go ritual and gave the box to a women's shelter that she finally felt she could move forward with her life.

For years, the memory would pop up, horrible and healing at the same time, and she'd wonder why she'd felt so driven to put herself through the trauma of hand-laundering those baby clothes. She looked at me, her hazel eyes like wet pebbles, shiny with emotion.

"I think," she said, "I was trying to wash death out of them. I didn't want anyone to dress their baby in a dead child's clothing."

She was also quick to say, "I wasn't letting go of my little girl. She's here." Nina placed her palms, one over the other, on her chest, then brought her fingers to her temples. Heart and mind. "I needed to let go of her death," she emphasized. That's an important distinction.

Letting go is not about forgetting or getting over the people we've loved and lost. A big obstacle to cultivating joy in the aftermath of death is remembering only the fact and circumstances of their dying, rather than their life and the vibrant relationship we shared with them. The clothing was a death reminder. Once the clothing was clean and given away, Nina could focus on the little person that her daughter was, her brief but beautiful life, and how her girl will live on in a different way.

Listening to Nina, the word baptism came to mind, not so much in the religious sense, but as a ritual. Baptism is a form of purification and initiation, a rite of passage to a new life and a new community. In washing the baby clothes, she was entering the community of mothers who lost children and starting the life of a woman learning to live with her loss. Nina's giving story, the reason she donated bikes to girls in rural India, was her way of loving other little girls in the space left by her own. It didn't matter that she later gave birth to two daughters and she'd become a grandmother, there would always be someone physically missing in her world that she wanted to keep alive.

As you know, you can't replace one human being with another human being. The loss is forever. Sometimes the hole it leaves in your life feels like a bottomless pit and other times like an opening for limitless love to pour out. Often, it's both at the same time. As your losses come along with you, the goal isn't to detach from the dead, but reconnect with them as essential parts of the invisible thread that is your evolving life.

How do you deal with memory and phantoms?

Memory isn't just a mental activity. Yes, your lovely mind can summon images and old stories of you and the people you love, but it's not all a head game. Memory is more visceral than that. It's why Nina had to touch and smell and see those clothes for a final time. Memory happens in your whole body, through your senses as well as emotions.

Maybe it's true, maybe the mind is everywhere in our bodies, right down to our cells. If I close my eyes and focus on my left hand, it can remember how it feels to be held in the warmth of my husband's hand, bigger than mine, palms touching, our fingers and thumbs interlaced, together forming one bear-ish paw swinging through air.

I'm reminded of a Vietnam veteran I worked with years ago who'd lost his right hand and much of his arm as a 19-year-old, but had what he called a phantom hand. More than 40 years after his limb loss, amputated following an explosion, he frequently felt he still had his hand. Beyond occasional twinges of pain or heat, most often his phantom hand behaved like a regular hand. He told me when his granddaughter's toy cars spun out of her sight, he still "pointed" with his right hand to look under the couch before catching himself and pointing with his left.

When he lost his wife to breast cancer, he said it was so much like his amputation. First came the shock and intense pain, filled by adapting to the reality of what was taken, the ongoing memories both comforting and terrible in her dying, and the odd physical sensation that she was somehow still with him. He called her his phantom wife. He shared that while she'd been gone five years at that time, he often sensed her presence and talked to her as he always had.

He asked her what's for supper, and she'd whisper somewhere deep inside him, pot roast and red potatoes or chicken and waffles, then he'd figure out how to make it. She helped him decide what to wear to a kindergarten graduation, and he'd tell her about the dumb things the Democrats were doing. For awhile, a neighbor lady kept inviting him over, and he grumbled to her about that. She gave him perspective. "We both had a good laugh," he shared, he and his phantom wife, and she chided him to be nice when he said no to the invitations.

He said, even though he'd lost his right hand before they met and married, so it was his left hand that had always touched his wife, he could still feel her with his phantom hand. With her death, it made even more sense to him that his phantom hand could reach for his phantom wife, holding on to her in a forever way.

How is that possible? Score one for the brain that, accustomed to communicating with two hands and discovering the absence of one, has to rewire itself. In reading about phantom limbs, the experience is often described as the brain re-membering the limb. The arm is a "member" of the body, so the mind tries to reconnect it, or re-member it. I'm a word lover, so I appreciate that clever analogy.

Score one also for the mind that is constantly trying to make meaning out of something that we can never understand despite its inevitability, dying and death. I think the mind, in remembering those we love, is doing its own form of re-membering to keep those we've lost connected to our lives and to make us whole.

Unleash your magical mind.

Do you talk to people who aren't physically here anymore? Good news. It's not weird or crazy, unless you begin to believe the person is physically alive or they start instructing you to act in ways that would be harmful to you or others. Up to 60% of people following a loss, if they're brave enough to admit it, say they've had some sensory perception of their loved one after death. It could be feeling their presence, or seeing, hearing, or picking up a scent tied to a loved one.

I hate when people call them hallucinations. There's a negative, de-riding connotation to that word, and I don't think that's what they are. Plus, what research exists to help us understand this apparently common process of sensing or communicating with the people we've lost suggests these experiences support our mourning process and reduce some of the negative or most painful aspects of grieving.

To that good news I say, "Hello Mama!"

For me, it's light and shadows. At times, I see pools of light that feel like my mother or my father. No coincidence I'm sure that these light pools appear during times when I feel a little lost or needy. Recently, I've sensed a low shadow that quickly slinks by, once rubbing against the back of my calf. Ruling out that it's Tiger or Chloe kitten, who are always in an-other room at the time, I think, *It's got to be Muir cat.* The shadow definitely feels like him. My husband was never emotionally closer to an animal than he was to Muir. I'm trying to make sense of these otherwise illogical interactions with a fleeting shadow. I can only believe Muir has suddenly shown up to comfort my husband in some mystical way as he approaches his own death.

There are a few puzzles here. For instance, I sense Muir, but my husband doesn't. If Muir is here for him, then why am I the one to know he's here?

I do know from being with more than a few people at the end of their lives that they almost always see dead loved ones. Oddly, they also see dead strangers, but that's another story.

The visiting of dead loved ones when someone is nearing death is usually comforting. My father, who was agnostic and still using his engineer mind in the final conscious hours before coma, then death, was analyzing his visions of people he knew to be gone but yet in the room with him. He also saw schematics inside the walls of his hospital room, examining the electrical wiring and circuitry. He even had an out-of-body experience, telling me, as he looked toward the ceiling, "I can see myself looking down on myself," then matter-of-factly commenting to himself, "how strange." He was simply curious about it all.

My mother was visited by her mother several months before she died. They'd shared a complicated, damaged relationship, and my grandmother's appearance seemed to bring reconciliation. The response was different when one of my sisters who died in the fire showed up one evening, my older sister, most notably to my mother without our younger sister who'd celebrated her second birthday the day of the fire. My mother was immediately distraught by the missing sister to the point of nausea, her body shivering, hunching forward as if wounded before my eyes.

I rattled through every mental drawer in my head trying to figure out a way to help my mother reframe her absent daughter. Then I calmly offered, "Oh, Mama, you know little girls. She's probably off playing." I looked around the room, trying to feel and see what my mother did, but couldn't, though I fully believed her experience. And no, it wasn't her meds.

Mama rested on the couch staring past me, her body and face relaxing, the fear unfolding into a peaceful acceptance that her first little girl was somehow there. I wondered what we looked like to my mother's eyes as we stood together. I understood my lost sister was still a six-year old, but was she as real as the adult me? I didn't spoil the moment by asking. Besides, what's real?

My lost older sister visited several times the next few evenings, still alone, and then the visits stopped as abruptly as they'd started. Each time, my mother focused on savoring her time with her little girl, who never spoke though evoked a sense that she was okay and felt loved. My mother knew the girls were long gone and that I couldn't see my sister as she did. We both knew it couldn't be happening, and we both accepted that it was.

Do I intellectually believe the shadow that's been stalking about the house recently is Muir cat or Muir's ghost? No, not at all. Do I believe the shadow is Muir or Muir's spirit? Yes, yes I do. It's a complete paradox.

Death is always one breath away, so life takes on dimensions that extend beyond the rational. It's probably some collusion between the brain and the mind to meet a need I haven't yet acknowledged to myself as I watch my husband's life wither and slowly retreat. Despite being the natural-science, geeky gal that I am, I believe there's something more, inexplicably and incomprehensibly more. If astrophysicists (did I tell you I have a thing for astrophysicists?) can believe in dark matter and dark energy, how they fill the spaces between the stars, why can't a shadow-cat traipse through the kitchen?

My littlest sister, who arrived when I was nine years old, also experiences my mother and father, though they more often take the form of a sign, symbol, or meaningful coincidence—all forms of synchronicity.

Synchronicity is when two or more events happen that don't appear to be related in any way yet combine to create a meaningful experience or significant coincidence. Typically, it's a symbolic number, word, or image that seems to pop up everywhere.

My mother was a dragonfly lover. At key moments when my sister has felt the need for support or guidance, a dragonfly appears in some meaningful way. It may be a big, green, prehistoric-looking dragonfly circling over her head or a slender, electric-blue Damselfly landing on her car antenna. It could be a server at the local diner with a name tag that says Judy, my mother's name, wearing a dragonfly-print apron.

My mother also appears to us through giraffes—it ties to a quirky family story about my mother and the length of a giraffe's tongue (which is about 18 inches, if you're curious). Once when I was lost and stressed, running late for a meeting with one of my donors and my mobile phone unable to grab a signal, I had a moment of synchronicity.

I stopped near an intersection to get my bearings and check them on an old-fashioned paper map. Glancing around for a street sign, surprise, I was almost to Judith Lane. As I looked for the name of the road I was on, I saw another sign, in crayon on cardboard, that read, Safari Kids Event, with an arrow and smiling giraffe face. I laughed, relaxed, and suddenly knew exactly how to find my donors' home. Of course, my mother would take the form of a giraffe to make herself known and calm me down so I could find my way.

Is it really my mother or the memory of her inside of me? Maybe it's longing for a helpful motherly presence recreating her. Does the *what* or *how* matter? No. Just as those astrophysicists describe space as curved, a difficult concept to grasp, I think of these experiences as curved reality. They are a gift and a tool that I call magical mind.

Magical mind is a great component of an Emotional Flak Jacket. I've known a few women who use their magical mind intentionally to call upon their lost mothers, partners, or children for help both in troubled times or ordinary, everyday dilemmas.

One donor I knew called on her grandmother daily to help with her pre-teen daughter. "Nana, how do I stay sane with this wild child?" she'd ask out loud. She was close to her Nana, caring for her through several agonizing months of palliative radiation that only seemed to shrink her grandmother's bony frame and sicken her more before she died. Past the deep grief, she still longed for her Nana.

Once, in tears, she moaned her wild-child question only to open a pantry door and have a box of Earl Grey tea, her Nana's favorite, fall to her feet. Synchronicity! She admitted that a cup of tea can't fix a willful, boundary-breaching "tween," then described how the tea's perfumed scent and spicy taste, the warmth sliding down her throat, helped her "chill out." She heard her grandmother's voice within, "This too shall pass, dear." Rejuvenated, she was ready to win the next round of verbal boxing with her daughter.

Memory artifacts and rituals help you stay connected.

Magical mind has another component to it, namely, the ability to use memory artifacts and rituals that further strengthen the connection with our loved ones as we become new people in their physical absence.

Whether a memory artifact is helpful or hurtful is entirely individual. Clearly Nina needed to let go of the baby clothes to release the troubling details of her daughter's death and let in life-affirming memories of her little girl's short but blissful life. At the same time, I've worked with other grieving mothers, and I've witnessed how meaningful a certain tee-shirt, receiving blanket, or toy truck becomes in their ability to create new lives out of what is often considered among the cruelest of deaths, the death of a child.

One donor I worked with for several months lost her college-aged daughter to suicide more than 20 years before I met her. Dixie was a stunningly upbeat software engineer nearing retirement who wanted to plan a memorial through her will and living trust as a legacy for her daughter. I'd never met anyone quite like Dixie. She had a heavy Texan accent, laughed loudly, smoked (even while eating, between bites), and when I shared stories about my organization's programs or tax-wise giving strategies, she'd say, "Got-damn, I didn't know that, got-damn."

We usually met near her office at an outdoor restaurant, so Dixie could smoke, but when we were finalizing her planned gift, she invited me to her home, excitedly telling me, "You've got to see my shrine room!"

As soon as I arrived, Dixie presented me with a brown envelope containing a copy of her signed trust agreement confirming her future charitable gift. In typical Dixie style, she joked that she's having too much fun living to die anytime soon, so it would be a long wait for her donation, adding she'd do her best not to spend all her money on cigarettes and dog food. Did I mention Dixie had five big dogs? Did I mention the serious-looking Rottweiler who stood up, paws to my shoulders, nose to my nose, greeting me a few moments later? Fortunately, Dixie's dogs knew an animal lover when they smelled one.

Dixie walked me down the hallway to a door, preparing me by explaining how she was "a packrat for anything related to my daughter." When she swung open the door, it literally took my breath away. The room was in part a teenage girl's bedroom, with posters of what would have been considered "cute boys" of the era, and part museum stuffed floor to ceiling.

Breathing in fresh air, I realized it was the only room that Dixie didn't smoke in. Looking around, it held every item that belonged to or was touched by her daughter. Clothes, stuffed animals, three pacifiers next to tubes of lipstick and eyeshadow, cassettes and CDs, newspaper clippings, clay, soccer shoes, blue ribbons and a plastic trophy—everything was there.

For the next two hours or so, Dixie told me her Loss Story and countless stories of her daughter and their relationship. The room was filled with Dixie's cackling laugh. I learned about the first book she ever read to her daughter and how she helped her daughter burn a picture of a former boyfriend in the bathtub, setting off the smoke alarm. She said that room was her "happy place." After awhile, she asked if I thought she was a "friggin' lunatic." No, she certainly was not. Many had told Dixie it wasn't "normal" to have her shrine room filled with her daughter. Not me. How can something that cultivates that much joy be wrong?

Do you hold on to memory artifacts that make you feel close the one you've lost?

I have quilts my mother made and a colorful, tweedy jacket that she loved but didn't get to wear before she died. I wear the jacket *for* her. She was taller than me, so I have to roll up the sleeves. On my bookcase, there's a plaque inscribed with Chinese characters that was bestowed upon my father for work he did in Taiwan in the early '60s. It was one of the few items to survive our house fire, though the card with English translation burned. Shortly before my father died, I asked a relative living in Hong Kong to secure a new translation. Not one for tears, my father's voice quivered reading the inscription.

Each time I wear my mother's jacket and polish my father's brass plaque, it's as if we are one.

Only you can decipher which artifacts help you hold someone close and which stir up past trauma. There is no one way to decide when to let go and when to let in.

I also have artifact rituals that serve the same purpose. An artifact ritual is a small intentional act that you shared in some way with your person, and when you practice it now, it brings your person to life, letting them into the moment with you. It's the opposite of a rogue ritual, which you want to let go of because it summons suffering.

242

When I slice open a cucumber, for instance, I make sure to rub the open ends together under water, just the way my mother taught me as a girl. She said it "gets the poisons out." I have no idea what "poisons" she meant, and I doubt rubbing the open ends together under a faucet would do much to render a toxic cucumber suddenly safe for a salad. I suspect this cucumber ritual is some sort of folk wisdom passed down from her mother.

Do I believe in it? Not literally. But. I consistently perform the ritual as a remembrance. In a flash, I see and sense my mother standing beside me at the kitchen sink, her long slender fingers in the cold water, the way she had her hair pulled in a dark, messy ponytail with baby-fine strands trickling down her neck, and her voice reminding me to "pay attention." I'm so grateful I paid attention—that's why this artifact ritual is so powerful for me.

Thinking back to Nina, I remember asking her if she ever washed her grandchildren's clothing. I could imagine the act would trigger that old grief, a rogue ritual she might want to avoid. Healing, however, is full of surprises. She still dumped the dryer fresh clothes onto her bed, the little shirts and pants in a pile. "It's okay now," Nina said, telling me how her "shadow child" helps her fold.

Review:

Stepping Stones to Help You in Your Loss Journey

 Sometimes you need to let go of items or rituals attached to the one you loved and lost, and other times you need to hold on to those items and rituals, letting them into the life you are building. If your loved one's possessions stir overwhelming grief, creating a ritual to let go of them may be essential to building a new life.

 You may feel your loved one as a phantom person in your life and find comfort in talking with them. That's normal and usually contributes to cultivating joy and well-being.

 Memories can be both haunting and healing. It helps if you can reframe memories to emphasize healing.

 Memory is more than mental—it's also physical, emotional, and spiritual. Your senses are a powerful source of memory and can be harnessed to help you hold onto your loved one, establishing a new relationship with them in your life.

 Magical mind happens not only when you experience the presence of someone you love and lost, but also when you experience symbolic connections between unrelated events or facts to support you, especially in stressful times. Magical mind imbues the ordinary with meaning. Magical mind helps you keep your loved one in your life, often as a perceived source of solace and wisdom.

Memory artifacts are items connected to the one you love that you want to hang on to because these items spur positive memories or bring a sense of their presence in your life. Memory rituals serve the same supportive purpose only through acts and behaviors that help bring our loved one alive in the moment.

17

Remembering

Memory is the wild place inside you travel
with care

You remember odd details—a speck of dirt under a fingernail, hands in conversation swooping through air like drunken bats, little splatters of mud on slippers, sewing needles and bent cigarettes, the red arc of lipstick clinging to the edge of a coffee cup. The quirks summon the person. You smile. Who knew the mind is a ghost house?

— from my notebooks, July 2004

Will you remember me?

When I've traveled in developing countries, I've been asked that question many times, but no more so than in Sierra Leone, where, as I write this sentence, there remain few tourists and most outsiders never visit twice. A bloody war and Ebola are harsh histories that take a lot of marketing to overcome.

"Yes," I'd answer, "I will remember you. Let me look at you for a moment, okay?" I'd turn my mind into a mix of microscope, telescope, and camera, looking, really looking closely, to "see" each person as the unique being that they are. I'd also ask their name and repeat it back to them.

We need to hear our name from others' lips, don't we? It's such human proof that we exist.

I call the process "memory-setting." It's part of my Emotional Flak Jacket, my mental gear, if you will, for being present with people and as mindful as possible in the moment. After so many losses and discovering how rare it is to deeply know a person, being intentional in seeing others and understanding what matters to them is integral, at least for me, in defining who I want to become.

Will you remember me? It's an act of love to remember someone.

As my husband's brain is affected by his heart disease—some combination of not enough oxygen, electrolyte imbalances, and bits of plaque that damage brain cells little by little—the ability to remember people is among the most poignant of his losses. It's not just a name, which is the first to evaporate, but the depth of his relationships—his life slowly disconnecting from others, the lovely feeling of love becoming muted.

Will you remember me? I've come to hear the question as a challenge.

You might be thinking, *Can't you just snap a photo with your actual camera?* Yes, when I have my smartphone or a traditional camera (hmmm, when was the last time I used that?), I will capture the person digitally, carrying them home as a semi-living memento of the people and places that touched me. My notebook is an additional tool. Writing about experiences helps recreate them in the future. But. The photo or notes are memory prompts. They do little to bring back the memory of the individual if I haven't intentionally embedded a memory first.

When loss comes along, memories are the most intimate stories that we carry with us into the future. Memories, at least in part, shape that invisible thread that runs through each of our lives.

There's a challenge, though, isn't there? Memories bless and memories curse. In cultivating joy in the midst of loss, we want to lure in the nurturing memories while disarming the harmful ones. Memory setting is great for reinforcing all the good in our relationships and holding on to the traits and beloved quirks of our people. As we go on living without the one we love, memory setting creates new stories to edge out the more harrowing memories that come with being a witness to dying and the hard news of death.

Memory bombs will happen.

As you dance with bouts of grief, move through mourning, and your days begin to take on the new rhythm of the person you are becoming without the one you love, one of the trickiest challenges to well-being are memory bombs. You could be having a very grounded day, then stumble into that drawer of baby clothes and be snatched back to intense sobbing the rest of the day, the week, or longer. Memories of your little one will flash by, a mix of fun moments playing and first words along with the grim details of her dying and the despair that she's gone, really gone.

If you've been with someone as they died, you've witnessed how their body and their face go slack. For months after my father died, and randomly now, I'll glimpse my father's gaunt, pale face in his final hours, his mouth hung open so like the painting, *The Screamer*. Same with my mother, whose head, after her last exhalation, tipped sideways toward my father, a single tear rolling slowly down her cheek.

The worst sort of memory is one that reduces a lush life to the morbid facts of death.

Maybe it's a song that ambushes you. I can't tell you how many times I've been in an airport dashing between gates or waiting to board, and then "Moon River" starts playing in the background. *Thank you, airport Muzak.* Despite a well-functioning life-support system for living with loss these days, I can't avoid crying a river of my own when I hear that song, especially at the airport. Not only was that one of my father's favorite songs, it was also, in a cruel-ish twist of fate, the song playing at the airport as my parents, along with my much younger sister and brother, boarded a plane, leaving California and me, as a 19-year-old college student. Yes, unlike other college kids, I didn't move away from home, my home moved away from me, thanks to my father's hard-won upward mobility as an engineer.

Tiny-Come-Back-to-Your-Senses Rituals and Joy Habits are tools to help you disarm memory bombs. As you grow your tiny rituals consistently, you'll be able to create some that you deploy as part of a protective, Emotional Flak Jacket, that is, a defense mechanism to safeguard and sustain your well-being and the joy you've been cultivating.

Grief is a necessary part of life, though nothing is healthy in extreme doses. An Emotional Flak Jacket can contain, shorten, or blunt the impact of the more suffering and stalling forms of grief.

It was 30 years after my parents flew away from me on that silver bird, and a couple years after my father died, before I developed a ritual that

I call my "Moon River" ritual: timed cries. For awhile, it seemed "Moon River" played on every public soundtrack. Now when the song stalks me in an airport or grocery store, waves of loss and longing washing into me, I allow myself a set length of time to cry, followed by a few "belly breaths" borrowed from yoga, and the word *enough.*

The first time I tried this new ritual, I was sitting in the Portland airport after a multi-day trip, meeting with donors in the Pacific Northwest. I was tired, missing my husband and cats, and desperately ready to be home. There was a live pianist playing between terminals, which made waiting endurable. Terminal is a terrible term for anything associated with flying, though on a long layover, there is a terminal quality to the waiting, feeling like you may never get home. Live music always lifts my spirits, so I was enjoying the mix of light jazz and sentimental tunes when, of course, the fellow at the keyboard started playing "Moon River."

My face felt hot, as emotion surged up out of my heart, which beat harder in my chest, a pulsing heat rising and filling my cheeks and temples, then I could feel the tears backing up behind my eyes, a pressure that had to be released. I looked around wondering if anyone saw me, and realized, *So what if I cry?*

I grabbed my gear and headed to a window where I could cry with my back to the rest of the terminal. I pulled a tissue out of my backpack along with my phone and set a timer for five minutes. I sobbed, missing my father, my mind flashing the memory of him doing a little jig in my kitchen once, then I was missing my mother, too.

Looking out at Portland's perpetually grey clouds, I let loose those tears and watched the guy with the bright orange wands outside guiding a plane toward me. When the timer went off, I dabbed my eyes, blew my nose, and took three deep belly breaths. Belly breaths are when you breathe in deeply through your nostrils, pulling air into the bottom of your lungs making your stomach puff out. After inhaling as fully as possible, you pause to hold the air briefly, then exhale slowly through your nose, or better, through your pursed lips letting your breath make a subtle, breezy sound as it leaves you. Finally, I whispered to myself, *enough*. So the ritual was a short but solid cry, followed by the three belly breaths, and the word *enough* spoken aloud. Guess what? I felt soooooo better.

I owe a debt of gratitude to Mitch Albom and his book, *Tuesdays with Morrie*. The seed for my "Moon River" ritual was inspired by Morrie. In the book, Mitch asks Morrie, his old professor who's living with and slowly dying from Lou Gehrig's disease, if he ever gets sad. Morrie responds, "I cry and I rage. I mourn. And then I detach. It's over; that's it; all over. No more. I just look back on how I've been feeling and I say, well, that's self-pity and that's enough of that for today." If you are looking for materials to create your Emotional Flak Jacket, it's a good read.

Our developed-world culture has a tendency to avoid grief, sadness, and crying in airports. But. If you never let yourself express and move through some of your most challenging emotions, that's often, ironically, how you get stuck in them. For me, the goal was to keep the memory bomb from pulling me into an inconsolable grief that would have left me struggling all the way home and taken away the joy when I finally arrived. By giving into the memories and acknowledging my loss of two people who shared a painful past with me, I not only accepted grief in a more controlled, manageable way, I also got to soak briefly in the love we shared, which is why grief is also good.

It is love's fault that grief was born. Who wants to live without love to avoid grief?

I said that to a colleague once, who immediately asked, "Well I didn't love my father, I hated him, so why am I grieving?" I'm not a psychologist, nor do I want to play one in my relationships. Still, I offered the idea, "Perhaps you are grieving the loss of *possibility*, the possibility for love between you and your father that's now gone." The death of possibility is a really, really hard loss.

After my plane, more like a flying bus, landed at my teeny, ocean-side home airport, I peered out the window at my husband waiting to hug me in sea mist, both of us waving to each other wildly as I stepped down the portable staircase, smiling.

Beware of memory blocks.

What do you remember? You need to know that our memories are not as constant and stable as we think. Memories can surprise, shift, and reshape themselves. As we work on becoming our new post-loss selves, the process of remembering can be a source of setbacks in much more disturbing ways than memory bombs.

Are you aware of memory blocks? The brain, as a protective mechanism, can block a traumatic memory in the short-term as well as over the long-term, sometimes releasing it months or years later in bits and pieces.

Women who've been physically or sexually assaulted often discover this brain trick. In the aftermath of the abuse, they may be completely unable to remember much if anything about what happened, only the enormous and brutal reality that they were battered and/or their bodies breached. I can tell you that losing a sense of safety, security, and the sovereignty of one's own body is among the most damaging sources of grief a woman can experience. If you are the one in six women assaulted, you already know this.

Memory blocks, while insulating initially, can spur internal conflicts. Beyond dealing with all the people around her challenging her about her inability to remember such an invasive, life-altering experience, a woman can be left wondering what really happened to her, as if she is a stranger to herself.

Then as she moves forward in time, trying to get back to a place of well-being, she may be stricken with flashbacks. Fragments of memory, intrusive and frightening, give glimpses of the attack, her struggle, and maybe physical and facial features of the perpetrator. It can be a mixed bag of clues to help unravel the mystery of "what happened" and put some questions to rest, along with episodes of reliving the most horrific moments in her life.

Memory blocks happen with all kinds of loss, and of course, they are individual. What might prompt your brain to block a memory, might not affect me in that way at all. What any one person can handle or endure physically, mentally, emotionally, and spiritually varies in wild, crazy ways.

With the loss of a loved one, memory blocks are more likely to happen if you were with them when they died in a grim accident, as a victim of a crime, or randomly in an act of terrorism, such as a mass shooting.

Alternatively, the shock of being told your beloved has died, even if to a terminal illness where death was anticipated, can induce a kind of amnesia that blocks that moment, that day, and sometimes days before and immediately afterwards.

Months or years later you can be sitting in traffic when a memory fragment assails you. The remembrance of the words, he's gone, and the physical sensation of losing your balance, dropping into a chair, and the sting of tears cutting down your cheeks can hit you out of the blue. It'll seem as if it's all happening right at that present moment.

That the mind can manufacture a new reality out of a lost memory is remarkable really, if unwanted.

I've had my brain suddenly release a jolt of memory, odd previously hidden details, more than once while on a phone call with a donor. Yikes.

254

When it happens now, I say, "Excuse me, an urgent issue just came up that needs my attention. No worries, but may I call you later?" Then, if I'm not in my home office, I find a private space to practice a form of my "Moon River" ritual or just breathe slowly, while my mind tries to unravel the question, *What the heck was that?*

Before I developed my Emotional Flak Jacket to defend myself from surprise memories, it wasn't so manageable. Do I take care of myself or not? If I fall apart or need to excuse myself, what do I tell the people around me?

A friend of mine who's an attorney likes to say, "Don't explain, justify, or defend." In other words, you don't have to go into any detail about your actions or try to rationalize yourself to others. For many of us, it's hard to not offer some excuse, but he's right. *Don't explain, justify, or defend* is one of my newest mindsets for living with an unpredictable mind and a brain that are always processing losses in the background. Remember: loss is a gopher always tunneling in your garden.

For many years, when a memory bomb or shrapnel-like piece of previously blocked memory emerged, I felt awkward or guilty, as if I was a failure at emotional recovery for needing to tend seemingly out-of-place grief. Then, if I gave myself permission to stop a phone call or excuse myself from a social gathering or pause to cry, I had to provide others a rationale for my behavior.

Those beliefs caused two bad outcomes. One, usually I didn't put myself first in those moments when I really needed to. I plowed through as best I could, conflicted, distracted, hurting, and ultimately pushing myself down a grief hole for days. Two, if I did stop and practice self-care, I later bungled through some convoluted explanation that sounded nonsensical. If nothing else, I drew attention to a situation that no one else noticed.

Take care of you and don't worry about what anyone thinks.

Will you remember me?

As years fold in between the time I was in Sierra Leone and now, I try hard to keep the memories vibrant. I don't want to lose the people who touched my life. Shortly before leaving Sierra Leone, I spent a few nights in Kabala, a small town in the northern part of the country surrounded by mountains, so slightly cooler, though still muggy.

It was the rainy season, and each evening around dusk there'd be a dazzling thunderstorm display. Low clouds the color of both charcoal and embers poured in as the sun sank away. The last night there, I stood under a thatched overhang at the guesthouse, waiting for the gush and clamor to arrive, enjoying the fact that, for the first time in a couple of weeks, I wasn't sweating.

Fanta, the maid and general helper at the guesthouse, joined me, pulling on a sweater. "You are not cold?" she asked. Still warm and sticky, I realized how truly adapted the local people are to their tropical climate that they could find a Kabala evening "cold." Fanta stepped next to me, shoulder to shoulder.

"May I touch your hair?" she whispered. "Okay," I answered, peering into her young, unlined face, her eyes so deeply brown, I couldn't see her pupils in the waning light. *What did those eyes see*, I wondered, *as a small girl caught in war?* Then I asked, "Do you know that your name is the name of an orange soda?" I told her when I was a girl, it was a treat to drink Fanta. "Ah, yes," she answered, smiling, "we have that soda here. My father likes it so much, that is why he named me Fanta."

She was braiding a section of my hair along my cheek. We talked about that orange soda, such an unexpected connection. We were both trying to remember what it tasted like. Then she asked, "Do you have to leave tomorrow? I would like to braid all of your hair, but it would take time." She finished her plaiting, as she called it, and leaned into my side,

256

sliding her arm around my waist. I put my arm around her, too, feeling motherly. "I'd like that," I whispered back, "but I must go." I was loving the idea, but I was also so homesick.

Quietly together, we waited for the rain in the growing darkness. Her sweatered arm, the heat of her body permeating the knit sleeves, pressed into me. *This moment is fossilizing*, I thought, *leaving its imprint in me*. I focused on every detail to deepen the imprint and set the memory.

Suddenly the silhouette of a fruit bat, several times bigger than the little brown bats back home, swooped between trees. Then up it bobbed against the last light of the day, a few feet from us. Its wings were outstretched and opaque, its face that of a worried fox, before it folded back into the night. The evening turned sultry and scented, a mix of green bananas growing nearby and the smoke of cooking fires coming from homes down the hill. One fragment of lightning flashed, then a boom of thunder, and torrents of water fell as if the clouds ripped, letting loose all their rain at once.

Fanta had to go back to work. "I think you should stay and let me braid your pretty hair," she said, her finger petting the fine braid she'd made. As she walked away, I asked, "Fanta, young lady named for a sweet, bubbly soda, will you remember me?" She laughed and kept walking without looking back, "Yes, Madame."

Review:
Stepping Stones to Help You in Your Loss Journey

 Remembering a person is an act of love—both love for the person and also love for yourself, because your lives connect through a relationship.

 Memory setting is a mindset where you turn your mind into a mix of microscope, telescope, and camera, and look closely, in as much detail as possible, to "see" each person as the unique being that they are and set them in your memory. Memory setting can help you build new memories to edge out old, uncomfortable memories while enabling you to deepen future memories and cultivate more sustainable joy.

 Memories bless and memories curse. In cultivating joy in the midst of loss, we want to lure in the nurturing memories, while disarming the harmful ones.

 Memory bombs are memories—both positive and negative—that suddenly emerge months and years after your loss, causing grief and sometimes significant setbacks in your life.

 Memory blocks happen when your brain blocks a traumatic memory in the short term as well as over the long term, sometimes releasing it months or years later in bits and pieces.

Developing mindsets and rituals in advance will help you avoid being overwhelmed by memory bombs and release memory blocks. Strategies such as timed cries and prioritizing self-care over whatever else is happening in the moment are powerful components of an Emotional Flak Jacket.

18

Meaning

Meaning-making is your superpower

To be a witness to another's life is to be a sacred space. Yes, you and I are sacred spaces, holding the ones we love. With each inhalation and exhalation, we keep their stories alive within our own.

— from my notebooks, November 2020

I woke on an early-November morning into the same uncertainty. *Is this it—is it happening?* I was listening to my husband struggle to breath, coughing and gasping, fluid in his lungs trying to find a way out and breath working hard to push its way in. There's a reason it's called *congestive* heart failure. After nearly three years in a downward spiral, these awakenings have become common. I know there is nothing I can do, at least physically.

Oh, how I've wanted to fix what can't be fixed. Do you know what I mean? Fortunately, we are more than our animal bodies. What I can do is be in the moment with him. I focused on loving fiercely, the way you might flex and hold a muscle. I imagined emanating empathy as a wave of energy, seeping out of me and permeating him, as if love and compassion could be companions for a trip he must otherwise take alone.

Each morning is new, but when the one you love is slowly dying, the only newness seems to be a mental calibration of how much more he's declined. Once again, air prevailed over water. He caught his breath. Funny phrase, isn't it? To catch your breath—as if it's a firefly or loose gerbil. Back to his raspy, rhythmic in and out, the delicate dance that is the miracle of breathing, my husband was able to fall back into sleep.

Sleep has become a cocoon from pain as his body literally falls apart, and from grief, as he says goodbye to himself through these lingering days. For me, the cocoon is not about freedom from pain and grief. I need to wrap myself around them, the pain and grief, to make meaning out of them, to be the cocoon for whatever comes next.

After pulling the comforter over my husband's shoulders, Tiger and Chloe appeared. They were hungry, and I wanted tea. They trotted at my ankles into the kitchen, then rolled onto their backs. They were two soft kitten bellies—my boy, a little leopard, and my girl, ebony fluff with nipples. Crouching down, I spent several, long, lush minutes, stroking and kissing and adoring them. Then, after putting down dishes of food, I listened to their frenetic lapping and slurping, their two tails, straight and still, except for the satisfied flicking at the tips.

Steamy cup in hand, I moved out onto the deck in the pre-dawn darkness for my good-morning-to-the-morning ritual. Taking slow breaths, drawing the morning deeply into my own version of a soft belly, I paid attention to how easy it was for me to inhale. As I exhaled, I let the air grate against the back of my throat, so I could hear each exhalation. In yoga it's called ujjayi breath (ujjayi meaning, victorious). Yes, to breathe is an underappreciated victory.

The air was rain-scented and fresh after a nighttime downpour. A partial moon muted in clouds spilled its light on me. Mist and the pervasive sound of dripping and crackling in the forest surrounded me, embracing me. Stepping out of the house, merged into something bigger than me. As long as I pay attention and be mindful, as my mother used to say, the world always offers some gift.

That morning I wasn't disappointed. Uphill there was a rapid staccato of panting hoots, then an intermittent *Who!* every few seconds. A Northern pygmy owl! I mimicked the call, and surprise, a brown form swooped over my head, landing in the redwood just above my potting bench. Too dark to see the owl, I could hear her claws scratch the trunk and scramble up a few limbs.

Pygmy owls are one of the few owls to be active during the day, often hunting near birdfeeders. *Smart*, I thought, *she's positioning herself for breakfast near mine*. They are cute and fierce, looking like a knob of bark only a little bigger than a beer can. They're hard to spot even in daylight. After a little silence, she offered her quick staccato call, then her persistent hoots, so much louder in her nearness.

Trying not to think, words nevertheless drifted through my mind. *Thank You. Safe. Here. Chilly. Hidden. Alone. Not Yet.*

Grace is for everyone.

It was then time to write, my favorite Joy Habit, my meaning-making version of play. Low music helps the ideas flow, so I turned on a Carlos Nakai soundtrack. You know his music? He's Native American, of Navajo-Ute heritage. The earthy tones of his wooden flute are grounding. Maybe my little owl friend with her flutey voice inspired the choice.

Randomly, the first song was, surprise, "Amazing Grace," not his traditional music, but then he enjoys fusing cultures. No words, just his flute and a background of strings. How could I not close my eyes and listen? Another surprise, I was crying. It was a big-tears, broken-hearted kind of crying. It dawned on me that I'd been avoiding crying for a long time.

My logical brain says crying doesn't fix anything, besides there's no time in the midst of my husband's dying, trying to manage all the details of home and four acres, juggling the responsibilities that two people used to handle, plus working. Not complaining, just saying. Too much crying also messes with my autoimmune issues—no kidding, crying can make me ill. Finally, I need to be stoic, keep constructing the version of me who's there to nurture others.

I guess it's fear that's prevented the tears, fear that I might not be able to contain them to a few minutes then move on. I'd forgotten that a serious but gentle cry is such a release.

The wooden flute played a slow, soul-stirring rendition of "Amazing Grace." The music entered me, infusing mind, spirit, and emotions. My animal body, ribs to wrists to ankle bones, all vibrated.

It felt good to let myself cry. When the song ended, so did my tears. Spontaneously I whispered, "You're doing good, girl, you can do this." Below or beyond the level of words was relief and a bloom of confidence that I would get my husband and myself through this surreal and enormous transition.

"Amazing Grace" has a surprisingly complicated history. The melody that moved me was not even part of the song originally—it came later, recycled from other hymns. The words were written by a guy who worked on slave trading ships in the mid-1700s, who apparently was such a jerk onboard that his shipmates shackled him and left him in Sierra Leone to work among slaves on a plantation. After being retrieved, the ship he was on nearly capsized in a storm and he suddenly got religion, vowing to be more godly, even as he kept slave-trading. I used to wonder about the word "wretch" in the song, as I don't think most people are particularly wretched, but the song's writer seems spot on applying that word to himself. Oops, a bit judge-y there.

Why did Carlos Nakai play me "Amazing Grace" that morning? My mind can't help looking for synchronicity, those meaningful coincidences between unrelated ideas like a smiling giraffe face on a cardboard sign when I'm lost. My history and the song's intersected in odd ways, for instance, in Sierra Leone. I recalled the people I met there, how I wanted to know and learn from them, and how kind they were to me. I'm an imperfect human trying to evolve. I couldn't comprehend the mindset of a slave-trading hymn-writer who stole human beings for a lifetime of abuse. Still, grace is, or was, available to both of us.

That morning, when Carlos played his flute for me, it wasn't just the song touching me, it was grace itself. While most of us think of grace in theological terms, it's actually a universal concept available to anyone, whether spiritual or entirely secular, without believing in anything more than possibility.

Grace is unconditional loving-kindness toward others and oneself, and it is amazing. Without grace, without that loving-kindness for yourself and others, joy is hard to sustain.

"Amazing Grace" is both a coping song and a coping strategy. The song was sung on the Civil War battlefield, then in the churches and fields where former slaves found freedom remained elusive. It was translated and sung by Cherokees on the Trail of Tears. It entered the repertoire of Blues and became a song of solidarity during the Civil Rights and anti-Vietnam War movements.

The most moving performance I've experienced of the song was by a Blues combo at Preservation Hall in New Orleans. The musicians were all in their 70s or 80s and African American. As they played, somber and exquisite, you sensed those men had lived through hard times and still savored life. You could hear their loss stories in the blue notes, the way they bent the tones coming from their trumpets and the slide of that trombone. When the music stopped, everyone in the tiny, humble hall sat crying—we were one body in stunned unity, emotionally drained yet energized.

Listening to my husband seemingly close to death that morning, in the back of my mind a voice warned, *Don't screw this up.* Even though there is no single right way to come alongside someone in their dying process, there's still the specter of regret, that I'll look back and feel I failed him, and also, me. Remember, the dead don't care, but a survivor does, and there's the rub.

Grace is an amazing coping strategy. I needed grace. You need grace. We all need grace.

The song reminded me to do more than cut myself some slack. It stirred me to project loving-kindness toward myself. I was doing my best, right? And you can't do better than your best. I needed to let myself rest in grace and have faith that somehow I will be and do all that I need to be and do for my husband. There will be imperfect moments. If you think about it, most moments are imperfect, yet here we are.

You're doing good, girl, you can do this. That unexpected phrase has become a practice during this time of impending personal loss and the isolation of a COVID-19 pandemic still out of control. For many years, the first thought I let fill my mind upon waking is borrowed from Thich Nhat Hahn, a Vietnamese Buddhist monk. "Waking up I smile. Twenty-four hours are before me. I vow to live fully in each moment and to look with eyes of compassion upon all beings." I consciously pull my face into a smile as I think those words.

Did you know that the act of smiling reduces stress? Even if you aren't happy, even if you are miserable, physically smiling points your body in the direction of feeling better. Smiling sparks neurons in your brain to initiate a chain of subtle but powerful reactions, leading to the release neurotransmitters and hormones—including those wonderful endorphins—that stimulate well-being. *Thank you, brain.* Are you smiling just thinking about that? I hope so.

These days, after I recite my mental vow, I add, *You're doing good, girl, you can do this*—it's a verbal vitamin to help me get going. Later, at times when I know the likelihood of stress or grief or self-blame is greatest, I pause to repeat the phrase, *You're doing good, girl, you can do this*, and add the advice, *rest in amazing grace.*

Are you being intentional in making meaning?

To live with loss and still love our lives, requires we each make our own meaning. Dragonflies and giraffes, kitten bellies, little owls in the dark asking *Who*, my personal vow and tiny rituals—they're richly meaningful for me, though likely empty of significance for you.

I'm not suggesting you try to make meaning out of the death of the one you loved, as in, *it happened for a reason*. That perspective is helpful to some and useless for others—either way, that's not what I'm talking about here.

What I want you to know is this—you get to decide what is meaningful in the day-to-day moments and details of living. More importantly, since how you spend your moments is how you end up spending your life, it's critical to define what a meaningful life is for you.

Meaning is a human feature.

As a child, I was told that what separates humans from other animals is opposable thumbs, our ability to grasp with our hands, which opens the door to many survival advantages and the evolution of our Homo sapiens brain. But. It turns out other primates and animals from certain frogs to koala bears have a similar capacity. Then you have my raven friends who can accomplish surprising feats with just a beak and clawed feet.

What separates humans from other animals is our ability to grasp with our minds, to make meaning. Meaning is assigning subjective value to a physical item, an experience, an idea, or another living being. We take a fact of life and ask it to represent something else of personal significance to us. Synchronicity and magical mind are elements of meaning-making, though there's more.

Let me clarify the difference between linguistic meaning and imbuing something with meaning.

Take the word *dragonfly*. We know what that means. We conjure an imagine in our minds of an insect with a longish body and a double set of see-through wings. We understand that word correlates to the living creature. I might even be able to teach Chloe kitten the meaning of the word *dragonfly*, the way I taught her to know her name and also her brother's. It seems possible I could say *dragonfly* as we stepped outside, and she'd look for the flashy fellow that she wistfully chases. She might be perplexed if there wasn't an actual dragonfly pacing the air above the pond, but she would associate the word with the insect.

However, could Chloe kitten look at a dragonfly and translate it to mean her mother, the way a dragonfly connects me to my mother? Could Chloe look at the dragonfly and feel her mother deep inside her, reliving her mother's mew and nuzzle? Is there anything in the universe, other than her actual mother, that would recreate the sense of her mother within her? I asked her once, but she doesn't speak English and just looked at me as her strange, chatty human pet.

While Chloe has an emotional life of her own—she certainly loves—I don't think she's a meaning-maker. For her, a dragonfly will always be something to wonder at and stalk with hope. Chloe lives entirely in the physical present, accepting and responding to whatever comes along. Chloe doesn't need the mental architecture of meaning to trot joyfully through her life.

So why spend time talking about meaning? We construct new, vibrant lives in the aftermath of loss by being mindful of how and why and where we're making meaning. Similarly, we can be haunted by meanings that we may have unintentionally allowed to evolve.

Either way it's a good idea to pay attention to the details of your days to identify meanings that support or block the cultivation of joy. Are there meanings you need to unravel, reframe, release, or revise?

Remember Nina and the baby clothes? The bits of fabric in the drawer were just baby clothes, but for Nina, they took on the meaning of death, absence, inadequacy, and even a kind of shame. Sometimes, once you realize the associations, that is, the depth of meaning that's so much bigger than the thing itself, you can resolve it in your mind. Once you see the weight you've placed on the baby clothes, you may be able to intellectually and emotionally remove it, and they can go back to being just outfits for very small people.

Often the meanings are so heavy and interwoven, you can't consciously alter them, so you have to look for other resolutions. For Nina, it was hand-washing and giving away the clothing in order to release the disturbing meaning that kept her lingering in the darker dimensions of grief. Eventually some other woman dressed her baby in that bear-eared bunting and flowery tee-shirt, and those clothes took on another meaning, likely one associated with gratitude for the gift and joy to see her own little girl warm and squirmy inside them.

Where have you assigned meaning, intentionally or unintentionally? Where might you make new meaning?

Are you letting your true colors out to play?

My writing poured out in the peace of that Carlos Nakai soundtrack. Turned down low so his wooden flute sounded distant, almost mystical, I could hear the lead of my pencil scraping paper. The writing, my Joy Habit, together with "Amazing Grace" carried me through the rest of the morning. I was blissfully okay, not the best and happiest person I've ever been, but also not the most despondent either. It was a good place to be when your world could change in a single breath, or to be more accurate, your loved one's inability to catch it.

By mid-afternoon, it was time for a light lunch break. My husband was settled in his recliner, with a blanket on his lap, dozing. The television blared (his hearing, another loss), and his iPhone was in his lap as he eagerly awaited the 2020 presidential election results. I can't print his opinion of the incumbent, only that he ranted that he didn't want to die with that man in office. I set a mandarin orange on the table beside him in case he got hungry, though his appetite was waning. Then I took the kittens into our deer-fenced yard so we could all get fresh air, do a little birdwatching, and see what's happening in the pond before I had to get back to my workday.

The sun had been dipping lower and lower on the horizon, spending the autumn afternoons in the trunks of redwoods rather than sailing above their crowns. It was a crisp, blue-sky day. The yard and pond were full of long shadows, making the redwoods seem like elders, wise and solemn, gathered around the kittens and me. As the kittens crouched in a huckleberry bush to watch Dark-eyed juncos, Chestnut-backed chickadees, and intermittent flocks of Pine siskins dipping down to drink from the recirculating stream pouring into our pond, I visually bathed in the colored light of leaves.

It dazzles my mind that the green we see all summer is a costume the leaves wear when they're busy being photosynthesis machines, turning sun, carbon dioxide, and water into sugar and oxygen—a pretty cool accomplishment for a leaf. Can you do that? I can't. The chlorophyll in the leaves absorbs the red and blue wavelengths from sunlight, reflecting back green.

It's not until the shorter days of dimming light, when they stop photosynthesizing, that the leaves show their true selves before they let go to wind and ride it down to earth. Oranges, salmon tones, magentas, yellows, chartreuses, peachy-pinks. "The colors feed the eyes, then the brain, the mind, and the heart," I said to Tiger. He chased after a bright, five-pointed Japanese maple leaf, swooping down at him like a little red hand.

I couldn't help thinking the leaves baring their brilliant selves are an important story. Don't we human animals often get so caught up in our own machine-like lives of work and worry that we don't let our true colors shine?

My busy mind was interrupted then by a familiar voice. From one of the redwoods, came a rapid staccato of panting hoots, then an intermittent *who, who, who, who, who*. The Northern pygmy owl was still hanging around! The cats heard her, their ears ratcheting back and forth to locate her call. We headed to the base of one tree and scanned upward. Yes, she was in there somewhere but unseeable.

We listened to the *who, who, who* call until it stopped. A large fist of brown feathers with a longish tail drifted out of some limbs in an undulating flight, then she was gone. I scooped up the kittens and hurried inside to tell my owl man about Ms. Pygmy owl. Tired but still with me,

271

he was happy to know an owl had visited and also a little sad that his days of probing trees with binoculars, looking for birds, were mostly over.

Then I asked how he was doing after his harrowing early morning struggle to breath. His blue eyes squinted and grey-bearded face tipped sideways in confusion. Turned out, he didn't remember the experience at all—nothing of the coughing, gasping, and frantic attempts to suck in air. I was incredulous and relieved for him. I was glad his brain and mind had made some pact that he didn't need to hold on to such an awful memory. *It's good practice*, I thought, *for when I lose him, for holding on to his memories for him.*

Review:
Stepping Stones to Help You in Your Loss Journey

You make your own meaning out of loss and grief as part of your mourning and moving forward process. If you don't make meaning with intention, you may inadvertently assign meaning to things and events that draw you deeper into grief.

By paying attention and being mindful, the world will offer you a gift every day—you just need to be open to the possibility so you can recognize it when it appears.

A mindset that includes encouraging self-talk and rituals around repeating positive phrases can help you push through tough moments or true setbacks without getting stuck in the darker emotions of grief.

Grace is a coping strategy. Grace is expressing unconditional loving-kindness toward others and yourself. Without grace, without that loving-kindness toward yourself, joy is harder to sustain.

The act of smiling helps reduce stress, triggering your body to release endorphins, those natural pain-relievers and well-being promoters. Smiling is a simple component of an effective Emotional Flak Jacket.

Meaning and meaning-making are uniquely human. Meaning-making is when you assign subjective value to a physical item, a creature, an experience, or an idea. You take a fact of life and ask it to represent something else of personal significance to you. Meaning-making often happens unconsciously, though you can do it intentionally as a tool for staying connected to your loved one.

 Often you don't let your true colors show through until some event impacts your life and there's a break in the facade. By pausing the work, worry, and busyness, you can let your true self, the invisible thread of you, be visible not only to others but especially to you. It's a helpful mindset for cultivating joy and fulfilling your Feeling Intention.

19

Practice

Building your Emotional Flak Jacket

"Your mother and I had been fighting—a little too much to drink that night. She went in the bedroom, slammed the door, then fell asleep in bed with a cigarette. I woke up on the couch as she stumbled into the living room, dazed. I got her out, but couldn't get back in. The fire was fast, so I had to come for you through the window. I believe I could have gotten them, too, but then the explosion—a can of hairspray on your mother's nightstand. It was like a bomb and that house like cardboard."

Thirty years after being a toddler in a burning house, I was listening to the heart of my father's Loss Story for the first time, and it contained a never-imagined, life-pivoting detail. I wish I'd had an Emotional Flak Jacket then.

My mother wouldn't allow us to talk about the fire, so we hadn't. Beyond my child-mind memories of that night, there were only a few conversations I'd ever been able to have about how the fire started. A grandma told me it was a malfunction with faulty wiring. An aunt had a newspaper clipping with a fireman saying an electrical issue sparked the first flames.

What my father was calmly saying was this: My mother accidentally started the fire that killed two of her little girls. Damn.

Living on the West Coast, I'd flown to Pennsylvania for a brief family visit. The afternoon before I left, my mother was away for a couple of hours. My father and I somehow ended up talking about the night of the fire. When he told me this story, so many thoughts filled my mind. Think, *volcano erupting*.

My father thought I knew, though admitted, it was easier to tell the kid version of me that it was an electrical problem with an old house, something a little mind could grasp, and he didn't want me to blame my mother.

When a loss has come along with you for a very long time, when it's central to who you are, and then it's suddenly blown open, revealing an enormous, if well-intentioned, lie, how would you feel?

I didn't "blame" my mother at all. I was heartbroken beyond words for her. When she came back from her errands, my father and I were out in the vegetable garden. Holding back tears, I wanted to run to her, say so much to her, but of course, I wasn't to say or do anything that might let her know we'd been discussing what was never to be discussed.

When I left for the airport, I hugged her. My mother never knew how to hug, limply leaning in as if she didn't deserve to be embraced. As I held on to her that day, longer than usual, I finally understood why she had a hard time being loved.

On the long plane ride home, floating in blue heaven above puffy, white clouds, fields of faraway crops and people, then mountains of rock and ice, my face was a ghostly reflection in the small portal-like window that everything passed through. My life had a new transparency and my mind raced through it, trying to make new meaning out of it all.

I thought of those tough, crazy years living at home, my mother drifting more and more toward the depression side of her bi-polar disorder. I sifted through all the hurtful words that filled our household, how I grew up trying to stay out of her line of attack. How differently I could have processed some dreadful times, with eyes of greater compassion, had I understood the pain and guilt that gripped her inside.

Back home in the West, new grief opened the wound of my old loss. I played my Loss Story and my father's over and over in my mind, crying and chaos giving way to calm. The sad truth of why it all happened transformed into tenderness, feeling the weight of the secret my parents carried for so long. Fortunately, that strange and necessary grief didn't overstay its welcome, as my mother used to say, describing what makes a good visitor.

Grief *can* be a good visitor. Grief, when it doesn't overwhelm, starts the process of making meaning out of loss so you can go on living.

The good part of that surreal grief visit: I knew nothing would ever rattle my world like that again. I'd begun to develop my Emotional Flak Jacket.

Do you have an Emotional Flak Jacket?

An Emotional Flak Jacket is a collection of mindsets you can assemble as you move through grief, mourning, and your process of becoming a new you after the loss of someone you love.

The purpose of an Emotional Flak Jacket—your mindset toolbox—is twofold. First, in the aftermath of death, it protects you from disabling, long-term suffering so you can live with loss *and* with joy. Second, it helps you grow your resilience, to be emotionally nimble, in facing the crises and challenges you'll inevitably encounter as your life moves forward.

I know the word *resilience* has become for some a cliché or even a negative, coded term. Resilience is often defined as the capacity to "bounce back" from hardship or tragedy and return to the way you were before the trauma. In some work or social contexts, it can be interpreted, wrongly, *as get over it, deal with it, buck up, be a man or woman, it is what it is, that's life,* and other unhelpful attitudes that imply some character flaw if you don't "bounce back" quickly.

In reality, resilience rarely happens as a "bounce." While we are a flexible species, we're not rubber bands (even they break with too much stress). More importantly, you can't truly go back to the way you and the world were before death or whatever horrible event happened in your life. You and your life may look the same after loss, but you and I know, they are forever changed.

Here's my definition of resilience. *Resilience is the capacity to keep on living with purpose and joy despite the many forms of loss and catastrophe that will interrupt your life.*

Resilience doesn't mean you'll be happy all the time nor will you magically avoid suffering. If you're living in a volatile environment—literal war or social conflict or destructive family dynamics—there will be limits to how far resilience can carry you without a change in that environment. Also, growing your resilience doesn't let belligerent or oppressive people off the hook for their abuses. We all share responsibility for creating a world where people lift each other up and everyone has an equitable shot at making the most of their life.

Everyone's capacity for resilience is different, because we start from different places. The good news is, from whatever place you start, you can grow your resilience by building an Emotional Flak Jacket that works specifically for you.

Let me suggest seven components of an Emotional Flak Jacket.

Throughout this book, I've described specific strategies and concepts, along with stories offered as examples for what does and doesn't work for some individuals. While I can't design your Emotional Flak Jacket for you, there are components that serve as the bones for fleshing out your emotional-support system. It's easy to underestimate the power of the seven "bones" below, to write them off as sentimental or naïve, but don't. These mindsets, with practice, are transformative.

1. Grant yourself grace.

Resilience starts with compassion toward yourself and then others. In the aftermath of death, you carry a kaleidoscope of notions and emotions within you about your loss, your loved one, the relationship you shared with them, and the kind of person you were, are, and could be. You may cycle through sadness, anger, regret, longing, and anxiety daily, or hourly. Grant yourself grace, that is, be unconditionally loving and kind to yourself in all your imperfections. Treat yourself with tenderness, the way you might care for a wounded animal, which, in the midst of grief, is what you are. Once you can regularly give yourself grace, you'll be better able to express loving-kindness to others. Then, surprise, extending grace to others will make you feel even better. Grace and lovingkindness also encompass gratitude and forgiveness. Where self-blame, unreasonable expectations, and doubt can make your world smaller and darker, a compassionate mindset is expansive, letting in light and peace.

2. Believe in joy.

When loss comes along, it may seem impossible to believe you'll ever feel joy again. I've been there, too. This may not sound all that sophisticated, but fake it until you make it. Until you *believe* you can grow joy and imagine life-affirming possibilities, it will be hard to experience either. Tell yourself, "I may not be feeling joy now, though joy will be a part of my life again soon." Repeat this belief statement aloud and a lot, until you believe what you're saying. Transformation begins in belief. Revisit your Feeling Intention frequently, too—it's another foot in the door to joy and possibility.

3. Breathe as a choice.

Are you thinking about your breathing right now? Inhale, exhale, in, out. Unless you have health issues or you're engaged in a yoga or meditative practice, I'm going to guess you weren't thinking much about your breathing until I asked the question. Breathing is the most obvious proof that you are alive. Thankfully, it's automatic, so you don't have to think about it, but that also means you can take your breath for granted . . . and your life. Consider this—the vast expanse of our universe is lifeless. That you are alive and reading this sentence is astonishing. Each breath you take in and let out is a tiny triumph over death, over being silent as a stone. You are here, and it matters. When you're feeling empty, confused, afraid, or otherwise lost, *choosing* to breathe and honoring your life force is a mindset shift that can help you move through those moods rather than getting pulled down and mired in them. Breathing by choice is simple. You focus your mind on your breath, simply noticing how it enters and leaves your body, and you remind yourself, *I'm here. I want to be here.* At times, you may think you don't want to be here. Again, fake it until you make it. Affirming your breathing life will help you want it. *(That said, if you're harboring thoughts of self-harm, please seek immediate help from professionals and loved ones—hang on to your one-and-only life.)*

4. Pay attention.

By now, you have a pretty good idea what I mean by pay attention and be mindful. Whether you're in hibernating-bear mode or chaotically over-striving, if you pay attention to what's happening in your body, tune into one of your senses, or focus your mind on the current moment, on something specific in your immediate surroundings, you can create a break from grief and whatever difficult feeling is rattling you. An extension of this mindset is looking at the world with curiosity and wonder. Remember, you can discover the extraordinary within the ordinary. The key is being open and welcome to surprises. Explore. If you look and listen, or touch and taste—whatever senses your mind and body want to use—the world will give you some glimpse of magic or beauty or humor or strangeness you never imagined, even on days when everything seems sad and battered.

5. Make meaning.

You are a meaning-making animal. Look around you or close your eyes and look inside you. Can you find one thing that triggers a memory or is otherwise personally meaningful? Some items or ideas carry meaning for you by accident due to delightful or difficult events surrounding them. Others are imbued with meaning, because at some level you've chosen to give them relevance. As you travel through patches of grief and mourning, identify what's meaningful to you—both in supportive and in harmful ways. By doing so, you'll remove roadblocks to healing while strengthening bridges to well-being. Living with loss is a balance of letting go and letting in. You let in by using the meaning-making muscle of your mind to bless things, actions, and ideas with significance. It's a potent strategy for holding on to your loved one as a life-enriching presence as you move forward.

6.   Love others.

Whether you're an extrovert or introvert, there is no "I" or "me" without others. You exist, in part, through your relationships, influencing and being influenced by other lives. During the deepest moments of pain and longing, love is there. There would be no grief in loss without love. Even if the relationship severed by death was a troubled one, the source of your grief still ties to love—the loss of the possibility of love, or more loving interactions, with that person. Who else can you love? Who in your circle of family and friends? What about animal companions? Perfect (or not-so-perfect) strangers? You can express love anonymously by thinking about specific people and encompassing them with loving thoughts for a few minutes each day. A step further is to aim lovingkindness or "positive vibes" at them through the universe or pray for an individual, group, or community. Going further, it helps to express your love directly through words and actions, and especially interactions. Being with others while holding loving intentions is powerful as long as it's mostly positive. Until your resilience is strong, it's usually better to aim love at difficult human beings from afar rather than in person. Also, because communication isn't perfect or always nurturing, let me offer a special mindset I call "granting grace-*light*." When someone's being hurtful, you think, whisper, or say aloud, *I love you, anyway.* Grieving will always have a solitary dimension, because only you know what you are going through, but you can't do it all alone.

7.   Get back up.

There's a Japanese saying, "Fall down seven times, get up eight." A big part of resilience is found in getting back up when you feel knocked down. I know what you're thinking, *Getting back up when the one I love is gone forever is the hardest part.* To keep trying, keep going, keep on living fully and joyfully, is the ultimate hurdle. It's breaking out of your emotional inertia again and again—no easy feat. All of the strategies and examples shared so far—telling your Loss Story, setting a Feeling Intention, creating Tiny-Come-Back-to-Your-Senses Rituals, practicing Joy Habits, and designing your Emotional Flak Jacket—are aimed at this most important outcome of your journey with loss. But. It all begins with a personal sense of purpose and belief that you *can* and *will* get back up over time. It's a mindset and more. You want to *know* it emotionally, spiritually, and even physically, right down to your lovely, marrow-filled bones. You *are* getting back up.

Let's do a quick tool review.

We covered many mindset "tools" in this section, so let me capture them for you in a list. You can integrate those that make sense for you into your Emotional Flak Jacket:

- **So what?**—Use it to remove unfair expectations from others or you.

- **The dead don't care, or the dead see the good intentions in your heart**—Use it to release responsibility for outcomes beyond your control or that don't matter in the cosmic scheme of things.

- **Reframe and defuse**—Use this mind tool to alter your experience of a disturbing memory by looking at it in a different way and taking away its power (for instance, reaching for the spicy scent of rosemary when the triggering scents of wildfire season arrive).

- **Living for others or being an avatar**—Use this approach to boost your sense of living with purpose and to remind you to balance accomplishment with enjoyment.

- **Letting go**—Use it when physical artifacts or rogue rituals associated with your loved one spurs dark emotions and pulls you down a grief hole.

- **Letting in**—Use it when holding on to memory artifacts or performing artifact rituals to bring positive feelings of continuing connection with your loved one.

- **Talk to your phantoms**—Use it to bring the love and wisdom of your person or animal into the moment.

- **Practice magical mind or welcome synchronicity and the unexplainable**—Use this practice to welcome meaningful signs, symbols, and coincidences that help you feel the support of the one you love.

- **Memory setting**—Use it to remember the details, quirks, and unique traits of your loved one and to form new memories of the living people in your life, which can displace old, disruptive memories.

- **Timed cries or the Moon River ritual**—Use this strategy to embrace, fully, feelings of grief when they arise, to contain them so they don't overwhelm you, and to move forward with a sense of well-being.

- **Stop for self-care**—Use it when a memory boomerang or shrapnel surprises you in the middle of your workday or social gathering—take care of you!

- **Don't explain, justify, or defend**—Use it after experiencing a grief setback in the midst of others—it works well with "so what?" You don't want to increase stress for yourself by requiring a rationale for self-care or worrying about what others think.

- **Supportive self-talk**—Use this practice in the form of repeated, encouraging phrases or personal mantras to coach yourself through challenging moments.

- **Smile**—Use this act as often as possible to point your body, mind, emotions, and spirit toward greater peace, calm, and ultimately joy. While not an immediate happiness-producer, it triggers a physical chain reaction that can lead to feeling better.

- **Be open to the natural world**—Use this mindset to stimulate wonder and curiosity that bring relief from grief while deepening your experience of life. Nature is available even in a city or suburb, for instance, by paying attention to pigeons, a weed growing from a crack in the sidewalk or a flower in a window pot, a line of busy ants invading the kitchen, squirrels squabbling in a park, and of course, any animal companion who lives with you.

Where do you go from here?

As you implement the process of telling your Loss Story, creating your sensory ritual, practicing your Joy Habit, and equipping your Emotional Flak Jacket, you should be closer to your Feeling Intention. Ideally, you're spending at least a little of each day, most days, experiencing your intended feeling as well as more joy.

How are you feeling now? It's a good time to do your emotional and your physical check-ins. As you practice these approaches over time, keep coming back to your Feeling Intention and doing your two check-ins to remind yourself how far you've come.

Let me suggest two next steps:

- Tell your Loss Story in a new way.
- Make a Becoming Promise.

Loss Story—The Next Level: After you have told your Loss Story to yourself, it's healing to tell it to others, especially at specific times when telling it unburdens or nurtures you. Perhaps you feel like you've told your Loss Story a million times. Maybe you still don't feel you can ever utter your Loss Story to another soul without crumbling. Past mourning, you might believe you don't need to share your Loss Story anymore because you're doing so well. If that's the case, I'm happy for you! As you live resiliently with your loss and with joy, you'll always be able to tap into the life-support system you've created when you wobble from time to time in the future.

Still, wherever you are in your loss journey, the death of someone you love is a permanent part of you. Most people find they will want or need to tell their Loss Story as they move through life.

What if you didn't tell your Loss Story but found another way to share it?

Consider sharing your story through one of the many forms of art, traditional or experimental crafts, music, dance or movement, written word instead of spoken, volunteering or giving, a Joy Habit, sketching it in the sand with a stick at the shore, or whatever creative process motivates you.

Using another mode of communication to express your story to yourself and to caring others helps you process and integrate your loss into your life at a deeper level.

Your Becoming Promise: A Becoming Promise is a commitment to you. It's a compass and a conscience through which you filter your life choices, helping you know when to say "no" or "yes." It's also a promise to others, because we're all entangled with each other, and your life always affects others.

Your Becoming Promise describes the kind of person you intend to become through your life, which is an ongoing work in progress. It's like a living epitaph. It's how you understand that never-changing, invisible thread that's woven through your past, present, and future while you and your life are, paradoxically, ever-evolving.

When you feel ready, set aside time in a quiet, reflective space and consider *Who* you want to become. Of course, that *Who* already exists because you exist. However, you likely haven't explored, then captured in writing, the qualities and motivations as well as the actions and impact that comprise your *Who*.

As you look forward from this moment, knowing you get to go on living but have to do it without the one (perhaps many) you love, what kind of person do you want to emerge? Rather than focusing on roles, professions, or skills, think in terms of actions and impact.

Start by making a list of the qualities or motivations you want to express, such as being kind, dependable, creative, ambitious, visionary, peaceful, energetic, or whatever surfaces. Then ask yourself what those qualities look like in action and what impact they could have in the world.

For instance, being *curious* is a priority for me, so I want to be a person who explores the natural world as the *action* I'm taking to be curious. Being *compassionate* is central to my sense of self, so I want to expand empathy and awareness as my way of turning compassion into positive *impact*.

Here's the process for creating your Becoming Promise:

1. Make a list of qualities or motivations that describe *Who* you are and want to become.

2. Narrow them down to the most meaningful *few* qualities or motivations—don't set out to be all things.

3. Determine how you will express those priority qualities and motivations as an *action* or *set of actions* you'll take daily, or consistently, as you live your life.

4. Define how your actions will lead to a positive impact in the world.

5. Write down your Becoming Promise as a brief statement, just a sentence or two, that's easy for you to remember and can be tacked or taped in a visible place as a reminder. Locate it near, or

to replace, your Feeling Intention, since living your promise will typically lead to that feeling.

Let me share again my Becoming Promise as an example: *I am becoming a person who explores the natural world, nurtures others along my path, and by telling what I learn, expands awareness and empathy.*

I'm not saying my promise is ideal or even good, it's just who I want to become each moment and every day until I leave the planet. Whether I succeed or stumble—and no matter what or who comes into or leaves my life—I try to fulfill this promise.

In crafting your Becoming Promise, don't worry if it doesn't make sense to anyone else but you. It doesn't have to be grammatically correct or a perfect sentence. As long as it encapsulates what it means to be you at your best, your *Who*, you'll have a promise worth keeping.

Finally, remember this question: *How do I live with loss without losing myself?* Once you have your promise, combined with your new rituals, habits, and mindsets, you'll have your answer.

Now, who do you want to become?

A Special Thank You

No one succeeds solo. This book was nurtured by talents literally from around the U.S. and the world, from Arizona to Michigan to Serbia to Argentina. I'm so grateful!

Thank you **Alejandro Martin** for designing this book's interior so the words delight the eye.
Thank you **Daliborka Mijailovic** for your inspired book cover design.
Thank you **Sky Rodio Nuttall** for your keen editorial mind and supportive feedback.
Thank you **Ellaine Ursuy** for being the epitome of an energized, enthusiastic book coach.

Thank you **Caring Tribe of Family and Friends** from so many places in life and time, who cheered me on, gave me thumbs up and hearts, shared opinions and honest reviews, and most importantly, in the midst of so much happening in your lives and the world, created space inside you to care about me in all my imperfection and quirkiness.

About the Author

During 25+ years as a philanthropic and end-of-life planning advisor, Kimberley's worked with incredibly diverse people looking for meaning after the loss of a spouse, partner, child, parent, or beloved animal to illness, accident, or traumatic death. Experienced with grief, she's an award-winning poet, author, and speaker on death & loss.

**Access additional ideas, strategies, & watch for
upcoming workshops & learning opportunities by visiting her at:**

PoetOwl.com

Help this book reach others
living with loss.

Please offer a review.

Thank you for reading this book.
I sincerely hope you found ideas, stories, and practices to support you
on your personal loss journey.

By leaving a review on **Amazon.com**,
you'll not only help improve future versions of **Grieving Us**,
you'll also help others experiencing loss and grief find this book.

Please pass this book on to others when you no longer need it.
Word of mouth and reviews on other reader platforms
also helps **Grieving Us** connect with those who would benefit.

Thank you!

:

Made in United States
North Haven, CT
24 May 2024

52902942R00189